The Pragmatic MBA
FOR SCIENTIFIC
AND TECHNICAL
EXECUTIVES

The Pragmatic MBA
FOR SCIENTIFIC AND TECHNICAL EXECUTIVES

by

BERTRAND C. LIANG, MD, PhD, MBA

Amsterdam • Boston • Heidelberg • London • New York • Oxford
Paris • San Diego • San Francisco • Singapore • Sydney • Tokyo
Academic Press is an imprint of Elsevier

Academic Press is an imprint of Elsevier
The Boulevard, Langford Lane, Kidlington, Oxford, OX5 1GB, UK
225 Wyman Street, Waltham, MA 02451, USA

First published 2013

Notices
Knowledge and best practice in this field are constantly changing. As new research and experience broaden our understanding, changes in research methods, professional practices, or medical treatment may become necessary.

Practitioners and researchers must always rely on their own experience and knowledge in evaluating and using any information, methods, compounds, or experiments described herein. In using such information or methods they should be mindful of their own safety and the safety of others, including parties for whom they have a professional responsibility.

To the fullest extent of the law, neither the Publisher nor the authors, contributors, or editors, assume any liability for any injury and/or damage to persons or property as a matter of products liability, negligence or otherwise, or from any use or operation of any methods, products, instructions, or ideas contained in the material herein.

British Library Cataloguing-in-Publication Data
A catalogue record for this book is available from the British Library

Library of Congress Cataloging-in-Publication Data
A catalog record for this book is available from the Library of Congress

ISBN: 978-0-12-397932-2

For information on all Academic Press publications
visit our website at store.elsevier.com

Typeset by MPS Limited, Chennai, India
www.adi-mps.com

To my son, Chris, who has taught me determination;
To my daughter, Kate, who has taught me humor;
To my wife, Diane, who has taught me love and dedication;
And to my parents, who have taught me courage.

CONTENTS

PREFACE

I have been a translator for much of my career, from the technical to the commercial and back to the technical. Jargon is a part of our world, and the area of business is no exception. This handbook is a result of years of observing and interacting with different functional groups at the team, divisional, and corporate levels in order to facilitate communication amongst very smart people who may live in the same world, but don't (necessarily) speak the same language. While explaining *corpora amylacea* to marketing staff, return on assets to technical experts, or the intrinsic pathway of apoptosis to clinicians can be gratifying, as a driver of our business processes, the interface and communication between the commercial and technical part of the organization has arguably the greatest value add for product development and strategic planning. Certainly, while many technical executives are well familiar with the slang of the business cognoscente, this book is for the rest (of us), who require a quick reference between (or in) meetings with commercial colleagues and need a guide to a land which is less than familiar and where the natives seem somewhat unfriendly. It is hoped that this handbook will serve to maintain a level of conceptual understanding of these business topics, and thus better interactions between the commercial and technical parts of the organization.

The handbook is organized into sections for quick reference, with an index to further facilitate access to areas of interest. The concepts and terminology represent the most common descriptive aspects of popular business concepts of today. Sections are intentionally short; descriptions are meant to be more of a *dim sum* approach rather than a full course meal; however, there are additional further reading titles listed at the end of each section with links to reputable websites and publications for quick access, providing the interested reader with references to search for more detailed information.

I want to thank my supportive family, without whom this project would have never been conceived, gotten off the ground, or been completed. My son Chris's interest in microloans as a fledgling college student, my daughter Kate's interest in science and technology (as discussed many times at the dinner table), and my wife Diane's newfound interest in business after a career in the medical field have been more than an inspiration. Thanks and love to you all.

It takes a village to create a book, and this one is no exception. I would like to thank my colleagues and friends who were supportive of this effort, especially those at Pfenex Inc. and the Sloan School of Management of MIT, who endured constant questioning and emails to ensure clarity. The people at both these organizations are the absolute best at what they do, phenomenally talented, and perhaps the smartest people I have had the privilege to be associated with. Moreover, the participants and staff at Sloan MIT Executive Education provided hours of interesting and relevant conversations and pragmatic issues in business to consider and address. For their thoughtful comments on the various sections of the book, I am particularly indebted to Ana Zambelli (Schlumberger), Martha Garriock (Cisco), Oscar Velastegui (Pfizer), Stephen Martin (QSpex Technologies), Al Hansen (Signet Healthcare Partners), Anita Liang (Air Force), Michael Hough (Advance Medical), Donald Rosenfield, Tom Allen, Tommy Long, Arnoldo Hax, and Roberto Rigobon (of MIT Sloan), and Lei Lei Sengchanthalangsy, Charles Squires, Henry Talbot, and Patrick Lucy (all of Pfenex). Finally, thanks to my editor, Dr. Scott Bentley, and the staff at Elsevier, whose tireless efforts made this book a reality, and finally, to Dan Bradbury, who agreed far too easily over a breakfast at the Coffee Cup "with the usual suspects" to write the Foreword. Thanks again to all very sincerely.

FOREWORD

When Bert Liang created this phenomenal handbook for the technical professional, it was a great service for every engineer and every scientist aspiring to a leadership position in a science-based company. But it's equally important for their companies — for _every_ technical company — because it impacts one of the greatest challenges we all face: developing leaders who not only excel in their own specialties, but also have a broad understanding of their total business and the range of issues critical to its success.

Technical professionals, who are really good at what they do, tend to rise in their organizations within the structure of their specialties. A molecular biologist, for example, might become the head of molecular biology, might even become the head of R&D. But as these talented individuals move beyond their disciplines to accept wider responsibilities — perhaps on a corporate task force, on the executive committee, or in the chairman's suite — are they ready for a whole new set of challenges? Are they prepared to make decisions in areas where their input had never before been required?

Meanwhile, the environment around us is changing so quickly that even our most junior executives must understand how these changes affect the overall goals of the business in real time. We need people at every level who can make the right decisions for the company at any particular moment, not necessarily having been told what to do. And that demands a basic business acumen, an understanding of the commercial and financial sides of the business, manufacturing and operational systems, human resource issues, business strategies, and business law.

This book is a fantastic tool in understanding these topics and more. From basic economics to portfolio management, it gives our technical professionals a comprehensive yet practical grounding in all aspects of business that a science executive (or executive-want-to-be) might encounter, and provides them with a strong platform on which to build. And I believe their experiences in going forward will be that much richer because of the breadth of understanding they will have gained from this truly outstanding resource and reference.

I can think of no one better qualified to author such a book than Bert. Because he is an accomplished scientist, entrepreneur, financier, and businessman himself, he can provide the holistic perspective that very few can offer. And if we are to create entrepreneurial scientists – a coterie of technical professionals who can build strong and vibrant companies by translating science into products that can improve people's lives – this is exactly the perspective we need.

Thanks, Bert; you've done a service for us all.

Daniel M. Bradbury
President and Chief Executive Officer
Amylin Pharmaceuticals, Inc.
San Diego, California

CHAPTER 1

Marketing

Table of Contents

"The best way to predict the future is to create it."

Peter F. Drucker

"Business has only two functions – marketing and innovation."

Milan Kundera

INTRODUCTION

In many organizations, there is often a distinct physical and ideological separation between the technical part of a firm and its commercial component. In part because of this, there has been minimal overlap between the respective units of R&D and marketing with a limited working relationship between the functions; indeed, this at times requires a specific linkage group to be established (e.g., technical support; medical affairs) to bridge the gap between these areas. Nonetheless, it is clear today that regardless of the strategic paradigm used within a given company, an organization needs be commercially focused, with a clear understanding of customer needs and wants, and with the ability to respond to environmental changes quickly and efficiently in order to maximize the chances of marketplace success. Arguably, an organization must be sophisticated enough to understand and anticipate the technical needs of a customer, and be able to provide solutions to those needs earlier and in a robust fashion in order to sustain competitive advantage. Hence, an understanding of the marketing function is paramount in the role of the modern technical executive (and staff). Indeed, the R&D executive may (and should) be exposed to various components of the marketing plan and strategy, including the marketing mix and microenvironment. These components of the marketing strategy, and the detailed communication thereof, provide an approach by which the needs of these customers will be satisfied, *via* responsive products having been conceptualized and developed by the R&D function of the organization, and offered by the commercial component into the appropriate settings.

Many studies have shown the importance of a strong relationship between marketing and R&D. It is also clear that often there is a distinct tension between such groups, impairing the working relationship and overall productivity. This "disharmony" can be a function of a fundamental distrust between the groups, and a lack of appreciation of the other's function within the organization. Moreover, this can be due to limited interaction between the groups during product development, with a minimum of communication, and that often occurring only late in the process.

In contrast, more successful efforts of the technical and commercial parts of the organization are a result of a '*harmonious*' *partnership* of trust between marketing and R&D. This can take the form of an *equal partnership*, where diverse aspects and activities from workload to rewards are shared equally, or a *dominant partnership* where one group or the other leads, but where there is a basic trust in the ability of the other group to perform their respective function – these relationships between marketing and R&D may exist with less complex technologies, lower R&D requirements, and/or in situations where less intensive customer interactions are required. Indeed, the more harmonious states reveal a significant value to the organization; most projects *succeed* commercially in one of these states, whereas in the disharmonious state projects fail over five times more frequently (see Souder, 1988)! For an organization, this very much suggests the need for the technical executive to actively manage the relationship between the technical and commercial groups, with frequent communication, monitoring, and understanding of the team dynamics, lest the multifunctional team go down the pathway of a disharmonious state. It is clear that the technical and commercial parts of the organization, working together, have the best chance of communicating the value proposition to the customer, and gaining customer acceptance of the product offering. Indeed, it is this alliance between the technical and commercial functions that is key for the company to successfully compete for the future.

MARKET SEGMENTATION

A market represents a group of customers for a particular product or service offering. Within this market, there are those who have the resources to transact a purchase or use, and have the need, willingness, and ability to effect such a transaction. This constitutes a *market segment*. Indeed, there are typically different components to a market, and one of the most important aspects for the marketing team is to identify those market segments which are attractive to pursue. The actual goal behind using a segmentation approach is to identify subsets of customers who will be the most attractive for the firm to create value propositions of its offerings (within the resource constraints of the company). By identifying these subgroups for targeting, a more homogeneous and smaller group can be targeted within a marketing mix (see below) putatively with a higher chance of success of being able to deliver a resonating message resulting in a transaction (*viz*. purchase).

The importance of market segmentation cannot be underestimated. It is virtually impossible to market a product to every potential customer by using mass approaches; the amount of resources and return on effort would be prohibitive. It is for this reason that the marketing part of the organization requires considerable time with the R&D group, as an understanding of the product characteristics and attributes provides a key pathway to develop the segments which can be served by the company's offering. Within this context, marketing teams will often divide market segments by four criteria, *viz*. adequate size, accessibility, measurable market potential, and unique need responding to a marketing mix. This is summarized in Table 1.1.

Market segmentation often identifies customers by specific aspects or components. These include demographics, level of income, lifestyle, geography, and patterns of consumption and behaviors for consumer goods,

Table 1.1 Components for Market Segmentation

Adequate size	Segment must be large enough so selling into this marketplace is profitable
Accessibility	Segment should be targetable with marketing activities
Measurability	Market potential should be measurable and comparable between market segments
Response to marketing mix	Segment is anticipated to respond to unique marketing mix favorably

Table 1.2 Examples of Characteristics Used to Create Market Segmentation

Consumer	Characteristic	Examples
	Demographics	Age, Sex, Marital Status
	Income Level	High, Middle Class, Low
	Lifestyle	Activities, Interests
	Geographic	Zip Code, Climate
Industry		
	Geographic	Domestic, Multinational
	Organizational Characteristics	Industry Size, Vertical Markets, Levels of Profitability
	Usage Patterns	Value Chain Position, Average Order Size
	Organizational Predisposition	Benefits Needed, Supply Policy

and geography, organizational characteristics, usage patterns, and organizational predisposition for industrial products (Table 1.2). Using these categories, marketing teams can segment the markets into a form that allows the firm to understand where a particular product may serve a need and thus create value. Of note is that *customer segmentation* is another term used to identify groups with similar characteristics, allowing a defined product to satisfy an identified need. There are many similarities between customer segmentation and market segmentation, with the exception that customer segmentation tends to be more granular in nature, and focused on the unique components of customer needs which are not articulated alone by variables such as geography, income levels, organizational predisposition, etc. (Table 1.2) but on *benefits received by the customer* (see the "Delta Model" section in Chapter 3).

Key points:

- Market segmentation identifies customers with more homogeneous characteristics with the willingness and ability to effect a transaction.
- Key components for market segmentation include adequate size, accessibility of the segment, measurability of market potential, and ability to respond to a tailored marketing mix.
- Market segmentation often includes the variable components of demographics, level of income, lifestyle, geography, and patterns of consumption for consumer goods, and organizational characteristics, usage patterns, organizational predisposition, and geography for industry markets.

ADDITIONAL READING

Henry, L., Razzouk, N., 2006. From market share to customer share: implications to marketing strategies. The Business Review 5, 33–39.

Souder, W.S., 1988. Managing relations between R&D and marketing in new product development projects. J. Prod. Innovation Manage. 5, 6–19.

Market Segmentation: Library of Congress, <http://www.loc.gov/rr/business/marketing/>. (accessed 16 August 2012)

Economic Utility

Within customer and market segmentation, the technical executive may encounter the concept of *economic utility*. Economic utility is the ability, for monetary value, to provide a product or service that satisfies a need or want; utility adds *value* to a product, and marketing provides key support of economic utility. There are five types of economic utility: form utility, place utility, time utility, possession utility, and information utility. *Form utility* is the alteration of raw materials and/or construction that creates finished goods. The marketing function of the company supports form utility by communicating the needs of customers to those within product development and/or R&D. *Place utility* refers to providing a location by which customers can purchase a product/service. Marketing strives to ensure that customers can purchase a product in the most efficient and convenient way. *Time utility* relates to place utility in that availability of product/service is present at particular times of day or season (as appropriate). Certainly, as an example, e-commerce has altered this component radically, in allowing consumers to purchase products at any time. *Possession utility* satisfies a need for ownership, and involves the control over use of a particular product. By facilitating ownership by sale, marketing engenders the creation of possession utility. Finally, *information utility* involves the communication of information to the customer. This allows the consumer to understand the product and its utility in order to make a decision about purchase. This has also been dramatically impacted by e-commerce, particularly given the advent of frequent and prompt consumer reviews of products.

Key points:

- Economic utility represents the value assigned by the customer for a given product or service satisfying a need or want.
- There are five types of economic utility: form utility, place utility, time utility, possession utility, and information utility.
- Marketing facilitates all forms of economic utility in one form or another.

ADDITIONAL READING

Padoa-Schioppa, C., Assad, J.A., 2006. Neurons in the orbitofrontal cortex encode economic value. Nature 441, 223–226.

Does Marketing Matter?

In some companies, particularly technical organizations, there can be some question on the role of marketing, especially for complex products. Indeed, at one company during its early stages, it was rumored that the product development head once quipped that the only marketing requirement needed (due to the superior product developed) was "a 1–800 phone number" (this company has since become one of the largest companies in its area, and has significantly more than a phone number for its global marketing operations). Arguably, the most difficult time for any company is during a recession (i.e., two consecutive negative quarters of GDP growth), where there is much more focus on value – and product purchases may be even more closely scrutinized. Evaluating the effectiveness of marketing in these situations can provide some understanding of whether these efforts have an impact. When assessing the effects of marketing spend on sales during the nine recessions from 1948 to 2001, it was found that those companies which at least maintained their efforts in marketing not only increased both profits and sales during the downturn, *but also in subsequent years*. In fact, even starting strategic marketing efforts *during* a recession was noted to have benefits on sales and profitability; a company does not either have to anticipate nor wait to the end of a recession to see benefits. These data suggest well conceived and executed marketing plans, even during challenging economic times, can make a difference in product sales and company profits.

Srinivasan R, Rangaswamy A, Lilien GL (2005) Turning Adversity into Advantage: Does Proactive Marketing During a Recession Pay Off? International Journal of Research in Marketing 22:109–125.

THE MARKETING MIX

There are a myriad of different components to any marketing strategy and plan. While these different components represent a variety of activities meant to bring buyers and sellers together for a specific transaction, they fundamentally fall into four specific categories. These categories are often referred to as the "*four Ps*" of marketing, *viz. product, place, promotion,* and *price*. Each of these represents components of the marketing strategy, particularly because they can be planned and constructed through a strategic process, like a laboratory experiment in which the scientist can control the respective variables. As a result, these components are readily and frequently discussed when formulating and executing marketing strategies for products and services.

Product

A product (or service) is often defined as that which one firm offers prospective customers or clients. However, this focus is a fairly narrow one, and does not encompass a concept of satisfying a need or want for a particular customer. Instead, the product should extend to that which offers a total solution for the customer; *viz. products are those items which solve a problem of the customer*, which is why the product was purchased. It is relevant that the customer perspective is the paramount consideration to understand what the product is, rather than what the seller believes it to be. It is understanding customers in a granular manner and matching their needs and wants to the attributes and characteristics of the firm's offering that articulates what the product is and should be (rather than the other way around). Indeed, factors associated with this definition include aspects such as packaging, labeling, brand, warranty, and service – each of which may play either dominant or minor roles in the product architecture.

Products will have a *positioning*, which basically is the concept of the product characteristics being stressed to the marketplace. Such positioning will derive from both the *primary characteristics* of the product or service (the basic features of the product) as well as the *auxiliary aspects* of the product (any other benefits of the product outside of the primary characteristics). Note that regardless of the product or service, there are both *tangible* and *intangible* aspects to any offering, and as noted above, conceptualizing positioning as *a solution for the customer* is the appropriate reference point. As a result, the positioning describes a *value proposition* for the customer, based on a careful mixture of the primary and auxiliary characteristics of the product.

Often, the use of the term "brand" is part of the product positioning and strategy. The brand (or branding activity) represents an identification of a product or service (e.g., by name, symbol) with the origin or manufacturer. It is a key item not only for identification purposes, but as a conceptual *differentiator* of one manufacturer from another. It also facilitates purchase by the consumer based on the previous experience of either the customer or someone the customer trusts ("reputation") that the product/ service will satisfy a specific need. Indeed, a strong brand can *per se* command significant value; the Coca-Cola brand has significant *brand equity*, in that in the marketplace higher profits are realized by the company because of the goodwill associated with the brand.

Key points:

- A product or service solves a problem for the customer.
- The use of positioning identifies specific product/service characteristics which create a value proposition for the customer.
- Brand is a key component of a product, and represents an identifier of the provider of the product to the customer, which can potentially encompass both reputation and goodwill.

Place

The manner by which products/services move to the customer encompasses the distribution, or place, of the product. The concept of place is inclusive of not only standard transport of the product from one place to another, but the mechanism by which the products move, where they are stored, how they are handled, etc.; anything that touches the product from its movement from the manufacturer/provider to the customer is part of this process. The compilation of these activities is called a "*channel*"; these channels are used to create efficiencies in the marketing function by minimizing the distribution costs of the product, yet provide the target customer with accessibility and opportunity for use or acquisition of the product. Indeed, the key objectives of place strategy are to ensure that the product is made available for purchasing consumers, that each component of the channel supports the promotional efforts of the product, that customer service is both strong and supportive of the product, that costs are minimized by use of the given channel, and that market intelligence is garnered by the channel, given the proximity of channel members to the customer (summarized in Table 1.3). This component of the marketing mix is particularly resource intensive, and thus requires considerable attention for both the marketing professional and the technical executive.

Within the marketing channel, there are a variety of groups which play key roles in the movement of the products from the manufacturer

Table 1.3 Summary of Goals of the Distribution Channel

Product availability to target customers
Support of promotional efforts by all channel members
Availability of customer service throughout the channel
Minimization of costs
Attainment of market intelligence about the product offering

Table 1.4 Categories of Product Distribution Members

Merchant Wholesalers	Take title to goods, and sell to retailers and other resellers (but only rarely to consumers)
Agent Middlemen	Sell to resellers but do not take title of goods (only rarely sell to consumers directly)
Retailers	Sell directly to the end user but is not a manufacturer
Facilitators	Support functions for members of the distribution chain, from collections to communications and transportation

to the customer. These groups essentially fall into four categories: merchant wholesaler, agent middlemen, retailers, and facilitating agencies (see Table 1.4). In contrast, distribution of *services* is different to that of a product, in that these channels are typically shorter and more direct to the end user, compared to a product channel.

The way that the manufacturer perceives the strength of the channel can generate certain incentives to move product through the channel. There are two types of strategies to accomplish this: *"push" strategy* and *"pull" strategy*. A push strategy consists of providing direct inducements *to the distribution partners* in order to have these wholesalers and other dealers promote the product further down the channel. Examples include *discounts* or *price incentives* to motivate the channel members to "push" the product through the channel. A pull strategy, in contrast, utilizes promotional activity to create demand for the product *from customers* or end users, in order to stimulate members of the channel to stock or move products through to satisfy the consumer need. In this sense, the demand by the customer is "pulling" the product through the distribution channel. Most marketing programs consist of a combination of push and pull strategies when considering place in their marketing strategy.

Key points:

- The movement of a product or service from the manufacturer or originator to the consumer is called the distribution channel ("place").
- The goals of distribution are to provide the target customer product availability at the lowest cost, while ensuring high levels of promotion and service, and the availability of market intelligence to monitor marketing efforts.
- Merchant wholesalers, agent middlemen, retailers, and facilitators are the primary categories of product distribution members; service distribution is typically much shorter and more direct to the end user.
- Push and pull strategies are used to drive products through the distribution channel.

Table 1.5 Components of the Promotional Mix

Advertising	Any paid form of persuasive message in a nonpersonal medium where the product/service is identified
Personal Selling	An in-person presentation meant to inform and persuade others to transact a purchase
Sales Promotion	Activities (other than personal selling) which provide incentives to effect a purchase
Public Relations	From unpaid presentations and stimulation of activities to managing the appearance of the product in the media

Promotion

Promotion is based on a detailed knowledge of the customer and marketplace, and represents *the communication of the product attributes and the value proposition to the customer.* These communications will inform, remind, and/or persuade customers about the product or service, using components of the "promotional mix," such as advertising, personal selling, sales promotion, and public relations (see Table 1.5). As such, the options within this segment of the marketing mix are many, and represent a plethora of opportunities and degrees of freedom for each product offering.

This process engenders a significant dependence on *communication.* There are four main components to this communication: the *source,* the *message,* the *medium,* and the *receiver.* In addition, two other components are important for the company, including *response* and *feedback.* When designing the marketing strategy, there is a concept or idea constructed to deliver to the customer. This idea/concept is then converted into a *message,* which is a constructed imagery (symbols or words) *encoding* the idea or concept to be delivered. The message is delivered within a specific context, by a *source,* which is typically the firm. It is the job of the source to best identify the appropriate medium by which the maximum number of target *receivers* will exist, who will be able to *decode* (i.e., interpret) the message being delivered. Once delivered, marketers observe *response* to a given message (e.g., sales) as well as attempt to solicit *feedback,* i.e., reaction to the delivered message from the source (Figure 1.1). Feedback is important in order to better develop messages that may be used to promote to the target receiver; however, as individuals differ in background and experiences, the level of decoding allowing for a uniform interpretation of messages is at best challenging. Indeed, that communication is further complicated by

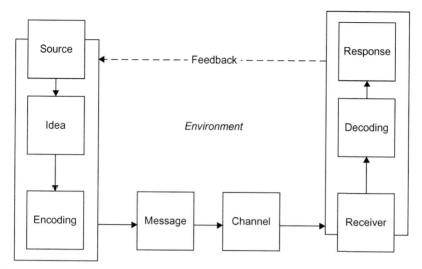

Figure 1.1 *Communication process for promotion. Source generates* idea *about the* product, and encodes *this into a* message; receiver *must receive and decode the message* to generate a response.

noise, i.e., any distraction, interruption, or contrary message that is delivered into the environment of or directly to the receiver. Nonetheless, well constructed messages may deliver the intended intellectual, emotional, and/or contextual message intended by the company's marketing team, as witnessed by successful messages by products and services in a variety of different markets. Hence, by being able to articulate the characteristics of a product or service which match the value proposition of a company offering, the technical executive and R&D team can play a key role in helping the marketing team in developing promotional messages for the firm's products.

Key points:

- Promotion involves the communication of product attributes to the customer.
- Advertising, personal selling, sales promotion, and public relations are components of the promotional mix.
- The messages delivered by the promotional activities must be clear enough in order for the receiver to decode and act (respond) in an appropriate manner.

A Rotten Apple: The Newton

In 1992, Apple introduced the Message Pad, commonly known by its operating system, the Newton, a personal digital assistant (PDA). At the time, there were several competitors with products in the market (AT&T, Casio) and others with products in development (Compaq, Sony). When initially launched, most industry observers described a mass marketing approach by the company, and while touted as being able to recognize handwriting, send faxes, and receive wireless messages, at launch the Newton could barely recognize handwriting and could neither send a fax nor act wirelessly. Further, pricing was set at $500, unrealistic for the types of features promised at even double the price. Indeed, the initial promises made in promotional materials around specific features that were clearly unattainable exacerbated the situation. Sales were poor, resulting in a relaunch in 1994, when the company attempted to segment the market more carefully (e.g., health care companies, brokerage houses) but continued to promise and promote a product that was not only unrealistic but drove early adopters to other products, or to eschew the entire PDA platform. While the price had increased to $699 (and later up to $1500) there was still inadequate margin for the product given the articulated (but nonexistent) features. It was clear that the initial challenges with features and poor handwriting recognition was a disappointment to even the most rabid Apple fans. While it was estimated that development costs alone were $100 MM, Apple only sold about 200,000 units, which was a fraction of the millions of PDAs sold during the period, such as the Palm Pilot. The disconnect between price, the promotional efforts, and product features, as well as customer segmentation, resulted in a disappointing product failure.

Rosen DE, Schroeder JE, Purinton EF. Marketing High Tech Products: Lessons in Customer Focus from the Marketplace. Academy of Marketing Science Review (1998) 6:1–17.

Price

The context of exchanging the offering of the company for value is the marketing function, and the amount of value is called price (see also the "Economic Utility" section earlier in the chapter). When setting price, technical executives should be aware of and consider a number of components, including costs, demand, and corporate strategy. Further, the type of product is important when determining price – new products in the market will allow different pricing compared to established products, while

Table 1.6 Examples of Pricing Strategies

Differential Pricing	Same product can be sold to different buyers at different prices (e.g., automobiles, airline tickets, new cutting-edge products)
Competitive Pricing	Pricing decisions based on what competitors are charging; can involve matching, discounting, or premium pricing based on product positioning (e.g., steel, mature consumer goods)
Product-Line Pricing	Using a multitude of products, maximize the profitability of the entire line of products rather than the component parts (e.g., "loss leader" pricing, bundling multiple products and charging less than the combined price)
Psychological Pricing	Based on perception by the customer on certain components of product tied to price; examples include "prestige effect": higher quality associated with higher price; "isolation effect": placement of moderate priced items next to higher priced items; "odd pricing": use of odd numbers (e.g., $2.99 vs. $3.00) to give perception of a less expensive product

products at the end of their life cycle and nearing obsolescence will have a different pricing strategy. It is important, therefore, to understand that the pricing of a product must take into account the product and price objectives vis-à-vis the other aspects of the marketing mix, and the relative sensitivity the target customer has to price (price elasticity; see Chapter 2 on economics). Because the goal is to generate a profit, detailed knowledge of costs and product demand are also significant factors in determining where to set price.

There are a number of different pricing strategies that can be used, depending on the noted objectives of the marketing mix. In all cases, the industry, competitors, presence of a product line (cf. individual product), value of the brand, and geographic considerations play varying roles in the determination of price. Table 1.6 lists various pricing strategies and their components.

Concepts around demand curves, and elasticity of price are discussed in Chapter 2 on economics.

Key points:

- Setting a price involves an understanding of both the offering and the objectives of the marketing mix, as well as demand, costs, and sensitivity of the customer.
- Various pricing strategies exist that are chosen based on the industry, competitors, product line, branding, and geographic considerations.

Overreaching in Pricing: A Cautionary Tale

On February 4, 2011, K-V Pharmaceuticals ("K-V") received Food and Drug Administration (FDA) approval for the drug *Makena*, for the indication of prevention of premature birth. *Makena* is a type of steroid (available since the 1950s) which has been used in the past for this indication, but was never formally approved for this use. K-V purchased the rights for the drug from another company (Hologic) for approximately $200 MM in cash and milestones, and completed a development program, using previous data from the National Institutes of Health, as well as additional clinical studies to gain approval, subsequently announcing a price of $1500 per dose. As noted, the active ingredient of the drug had been available previously by *compounding pharmacies*; it was sold *prior to Makena's* approval at *$15 a dose*. The company sent letters to the compounding pharmacies who had previously sold the drug noting that the FDA could enforce actions against them, since there was now an approved drug (customarily the case). However, with the announcement of *Makena's* price, patients, doctors, NGOs, and government representatives expressed outrage with the company, with senators and congressmen calling for investigations by both the trade and reimbursement arms of the Federal Government. Presumably in response to this turmoil, the FDA then publically announced that, as opposed to the usual practice, it *would allow* the compounding pharmacies to continue to formulate and make available the drug as they had in the past. Insurance companies encouraged patients and doctors to use the compounded pharmacy product rather than *Makena*. With such pressure, K-V was effectively forced to reduce the price (by over 50%), and revamp its revenue and business model going forward.

ADDITIONAL READING

Henry, L., Razzouk, N., 2006. From market share to customer share: implications to marketing strategies. The Business Review 5, 33–39.

Shapiro, B.P., 1985. Rejuvenating the marketing mix. Harv. Bus. Rev. September/October, 28–34.

GENERAL REFERENCES AND WEBSITES RELATED TO MARKETING

Mullins, J., Walker, O., Boyd, H., 2009. Marketing Management: A Strategic Decision-Making Approach. Irwin McGraw-Hill, Boston.

Zikmund, W.G., d'Amico, M., 2002. Effective Marketing: Creating and Keeping Customers in an E-commerce World, third ed. South-Western, New York.

American Marketing Association, <http://www.marketingpower.com/ResourceLibrary/Pages/default.aspx>. (accessed 16 August 2012)

All About Marketing, <http://managementhelp.org/marketing/index.htm>. (accessed 16 August 2012)

Economics

Table of Contents

"For an economist the real world is often a special case."

Edgar R. Fiedler

"Unfortunately, theory is silent on exactly when the long run arrives."

Sam Peltzman

INTRODUCTION

An understanding of economics is important for the technical executive, as decisions influenced by changes in both micro- and macroeconomic indicators have direct implications on costs, as well as markets, both domestically and abroad. Specifically, issues around demand, interest rates, outputs of countries, inflation, and exchange rates will no doubt enter into corporate conversations when making decisions to enter or sell to companies or consumers domiciled in regions outside the domestic borders of the firm. Moreover, purchasing patterns for supplies and services from other countries relate to specific aspects of economics, and have direct effects on budgeting and financing decisions in all business units of the company. An understanding of such concepts will allow executives in the

The Pragmatic MBA for Scientific and Technical Executives
DOI: http://dx.doi.org/10.1016/B978-0-12-397932-2.00002-8

R&D function to better understand the ramifications of buying from or selling to entities abroad, facilitating decisions and the timing of such decisions for the advantage of the firm.

MARKETS
Supply and Demand

Microeconomic assessments of markets revolve around product or service offerings being bought by those with the "power" (e.g., resources) to purchase; it is the economic model of supply and demand. Without question, concepts about markets are relevant to technical (and other) executives who face the day-to-day requirement of generating value for the firm, and making decisions on resource allocation to product and/or service offerings, given a specific demand. In general, this model posits there is a price of a particular product/service where the quantity demanded will equal the quantity supplied by all producers (assuming a competitive marketplace), resulting in an *equilibrium* of price and quantity. This market behavior is based on the idea that changes in either demand or supply will modify the price and quantity at which equilibrium occurs. This assumes that increases in demand are associated with an increase in price, given a constant supply ("a higher equilibrium point of price and quantity"), while lower demand with constant supply result in a decrease in price and quantity equilibrium. Similarly, increases in supply with constant demand results in lower equilibrium price at higher quantity, and lower supply given constant demand results in higher price and lower quantity. Table 2.1 summarizes these assumptions, and Figure 2.1 shows the demand (conceptualized as a price-quantity) curve.

Markets are also described as being "efficient," in that the allocation of goods and services are both dynamic and self-correcting. The ability of sellers of goods and services to *create change in the marketplace* (i.e., introduce new goods or services) is easily facilitated; the ability to introduce new goods at a given price (dynamic) allows a supplier to begin to establish the equilibrium position without any monolithic authoritarian structures as a *sine qua non*. Moreover, price establishes the hurdle by which purchasers will or will not exercise the power to buy; if there is a low (or no) amount of purchasing (i.e. low or no demand), price will adjust ("self-correct") in order to meet the needs of the marketplace. While markets and competitors are indeed not perfect, and interventions by governments and market influence by suppliers exist, the economic model of supply

Table 2.1 Supply and Demand Scenarios

Supply	Demand	Result
Unchanged	Increase	Higher equilibrium price and quantity
Unchanged	Decrease	Lower equilibrium price and quantity
Increase	Unchanged	Lower equilibrium price and higher quantity
Decrease	Unchanged	Higher equilibrium price and lower quantity

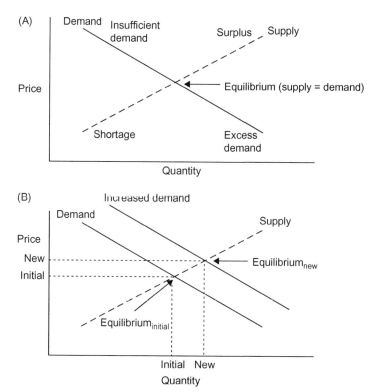

Figure 2.1 *Demand Curve.* (A) Standard demand curve; note equilibrium point, where supply equals demand. (B) Example of increased demand, establishing new equilibrium point, and therefore increased quantity supplied and price at equilibrium. Similar movement of either of the curves higher or lower will result in new equilibrium points, and thus price and quantity amounts. Also see Table 2.1.

and demand provides the paradigm by which most firms are guided when considering their respective value chains and products.

Key points:

- The supply and demand economic model describes the interaction between suppliers and buyers which thereby determines price.
- Equilibrium in supply and demand encompass a given price and quantity to be supplied to the marketplace.
- Changes in equilibrium occur when either/both supply and demand change, thus changing price and quantity.

Supply and Demand: Tickle-Me-Elmo

In 1996, Tyco Preschool released a toy for the anticipated holiday season, *Tickle-Me-Elmo*. The toy was based on the popular Sesame Street television show character, Elmo the Monster. When squeezed, the toy would make a laughing sound, and when squeezed three times in a row, it would laugh and vibrate. The toy had unprecedented (and unanticipated) demand, becoming a huge fad. There were soon shortages across the country as demand far outstripped supply; at times, violence erupted between customers attempting to purchase the limited numbers of toys available, and clerks became injured when attempting to pacify customers or put out new displays.

The toy originally sold for $28.99, but during the height of the shortage, and proximity to Christmas, prices as high as $1500 were advertised (and paid) by buyers "desperate" for the toy.

Dean, Katie. Elmo's Worth More than a Tickle. Wired. October 11, 2001.

ADDITIONAL READING

Nicholson, W., Snyder, C., 2008. Microeconomic Theory: Basic Principles and Extensions, tenth ed. Thomson South-Western, Mason.

Prasch, R.E., 2008. How Markets Work: Supply, Demand and the 'Real World.' Edward Elgar, Northampton.

Sachdev, A. (2009, September 29) New tenet in law of supply and demand. Chicago Tribune.

Elasticity

Price elasticity is the measure of the responsiveness of sales to a change in the price of a product. In general, price elasticity is useful because it may assist a firm in understanding the relative changes in demand curves and relative margins/revenues given alterations in price (price elasticity of demand); similarly, it can also predict how the quantity supplied will be altered by changes in price (price elasticity of supply). By understanding these factors, a company can estimate the effects of price increases (with associated decreases in demand but increase revenues per SKU) or external alterations in price (e.g., by tariffs, distribution costs, etc.). The standard formula for calculating price elasticity of demand (supply) is (using absolute, i.e., nonnegative numbers)

$$\text{Elasticity} = \% \text{ change in quantity demanded}$$
$$(\text{or supplied}) / \% \text{ change in price}$$

In general, if the *elasticity calculated is greater than 1* (i.e., percentage change in quantity/supply is greater than the percentage change in price), the demand or supply is considered to be *elastic* (*demand/supply is sensitive to changes in price*). Similarly, if the calculated elasticity is *less than 1*, then the demand or supply is considered to be *inelastic* (i.e., *changes in price have only a small effect on quantity demanded/supplied*). In terms of demand, inelastic items are usually *necessities* (e.g., milk, or clean drinking water, particularly during a crisis such as the Japanese Fukushima catastrophe in 2011) while elastic items are those which may have adequate substitutes (e.g., television *vs.* $2000 Stanley Cup Game 7 tickets, presuming one is not a fan of the teams playing). At the extreme, when there is perfectly inelastic supply (no change in quantity supplied with a change in price), elasticity is 0, and the quantity supplied is a vertical line in the demand curve (see Figure 2.1); hence, decreases in demand will directly result in decreases in price at equilibrium, and increases in demand will result in increases in equilibrium price. In this case, supply cannot meet a change in demand (no excess capacity). An example of this is a rare car, like a gullwing 300SL Mercedes-Benz; any increase in price does not change the quantity supplied. The converse case, where there is perfectly elastic supply, would be a horizontal line in the demand curve. Here, supply can react quickly to changes in demand, *viz.* there is excess capacity; an (imperfect) example of this is an empty restaurant. Such examples illustrate responsiveness of the consumer and producer in different situations.

Key points:

- Elasticity is a measure of changes in demand or supply with a change in price.
- An elasticity greater than one indicates an elastic product/service, while an elasticity less than 1 is inelastic.

ADDITIONAL READING

Ellison, G., Ellison, S.F., 2009. Search, obfuscation, and price elasticities on the Internet. Econometrica 2, 427–452.

Ringel, J.S., Hosek, S.D., Vollaard, B.A., Mahnovski, S., 2005. National Defense Research
    Institute RAND Health. The Elasticity of Demand for Health Care.
Price Elasticity of Demand, <http://www.mackinac.org/1247>. (accessed 17 August 2012)

GROSS DOMESTIC PRODUCT

As opposed to microeconomics, which concerns itself with market behavior of firms and individual consumers, macroeconomics is the study of an economy in aggregate, such as a national economy. The gross domestic product of a country (GDP) represents the overall value of final goods and services produced by a given country's economy over a given period of time. As such, it includes both consumer goods and investment goods (also known as capital goods) and human capital, and is a (very) rough estimate of the standard of living of a country. While the two categories of consumer and investment goods are important in the conceptualization of GDP, there are several ways to actually measure or determine GDP. These include the product (output) approach, the income approach, and the expenditure approach. Of importance is that each of these methods essentially provides the same information in different ways; and while perhaps not exact, they are coincident upon general values that can be used for comparison within and between countries. Table 2.2 shows the main considerations of each assessment. Indeed, these formulas have very similar components, in that consumer goods (which describes consumption by the nation's households) and investment goods/outputs (supporting capital wealth of the country), in addition to governmental accounts, play key roles in all of the GDP calculations. All are obviously imperative in the support of the overall economic well-being of a country.

It must be emphasized that the GDP only refers to *finished goods*; unfinished goods are not part of the calculation in any of the noted systems.

There are obviously limitations to the GDP. Year-on-year comparisons must take into account changes in the value of money (i.e., inflation, deflation) and are usually normalized to a specific year; the calculation does not account for changes in the types of goods and services; wasteful or inefficient production are included in the calculation; distribution of production is not accounted for; there is no accounting for disparity of incomes; nonmarket transactions are not measured; there are no measures of sustainability of growth; etc. Hence, using GDP alone as an estimation of standard of living is at best flawed. Nonetheless, while there are

Table 2.2 Calculation of GDP

Product (Output) GDP	The sum of all outputs from every class of business in a country: Private Consumption + Gross Investments + Government Spending + (Exports − Imports)
Expenditure GDP	The sum of all expenditures made in purchasing items in a country: Final Consumption Expenditure (Private and Government) + Investment Expenditure + (Exports − Imports)
Income GDP	The sum of all incomes of productive factors in a country: Wages + Rent + Interest + Gross Profits + (Indirect Taxes − Subsidies) + Depreciation

challenges to the specific measures of GDP, its value is as *a broad economic indicator showing a level of activity of an economy*. This, combined with an understanding of both exchange rates and purchasing power parity allows companies and executives to estimate diverse considerations important to a company, including investments in tangible infrastructure, market sizes, price parity, or sourcing.

Key points:

- GDP (particularly changes in GDP) is an indicator of the standard of living in a given country.
- GDP reflects the outputs of an economy for a country over a specific time period.
- GDP only reflects finished products which have undergone market transactions.

Are There Alternatives to GDP?

As noted, the GDP as a measure of standard of living and economic progress is at best limited. However, many economists are hesitant to replace or even modify the GDP because of the difficulty in quantification and objectively measuring impact of such a change. While measures of national progress in living standards and economic growth have increased over the past several years (e.g., Index of Sustainable Economic Welfare, Genuine Progress Indicator, Human Development Index, Happy Planet Index), none have necessarily been demonstrated to be a better index that might replace the GDP in assessment of a country's economic status. Hence, despite all its limitations, GDP (and GDP/capita) continues to be a well-documented general measure of economic status, particularly over time.

ADDITIONAL READING

Steven, L.J., Seskin, E.P., Fraumeni, B.M., 2008. Taking the pulse of the economy: measuring GDP. J. Econ. Perspect. 22, 193–216.
Bureau of Economic Analysis, <http://www.bea.gov/index.htm>. (accessed 20 August 2012)
Field Listing: GDP (Official Fact Book), <https://www.cia.gov/library/publications/the-world-factbook/fields/2195.html>. (accessed 20 August 2012)

INFLATION

Inflation represents the *ongoing change (increases) of prices over time*, thus determining the power of the currency for purchasing. While inflation is of key concern to executives on a domestic basis, it is also important for a firm that does business in other countries or sources materials abroad, due to the intricate relationship between exchange and interest rates (see below). In the U.S., inflation is measured using the Consumer Price Index (CPI), which is reported monthly. Recently, a more detailed effort to measure inflation by collecting prices from literally millions of sources, encompassing many different countries, has been established at MIT (Billion Prices Project, PriceStats, bpp.mit.edu) and represents a daily evaluation of prices to reflect inflation rates. In contrast, the CPI measures a "basket of goods and services" reflective of the U.S.; similar (but not exact) baskets are measured in different countries around the world to calculate domestic inflation rates; such evaluations have widely variable results, but can provide a guide to the relative level of price changes with time.

While the causes of inflation are complex, fundamentally it is due to *an increase of currency supply at a faster rate than the demand* for that currency. Central banks (for example, the Federal Reserve) tend to control inflation by *controlling the money supply*; the mechanisms used include controlling the discount rate (the rate banks can borrow reserves from the Federal Reserve), changing reserve requirements of banks (increase money supply by lowering reserve requirements; decrease money supply by increasing reserve requirements), and buying bonds in the open market (increasing money into the commercial bank coffers available for lending). Thus, the Federal Reserve can control the money supply and discount rate (directly); of note, however, is that the control of interest rates charged by commercial banks is *not* under central bank control, at least not directly.

Inflation has significant implications for businesses, of which the technical executive should be aware. Because credit holders can pay back liabilities with less valuable dollars, *higher inflation* can reduce the overall value of capital at the expense of the lender; this obviously works both for (based on accounts payable and loans) and against (based on revenues received as well as accounts receivable) the company. On the other hand, with *lower inflation*, the converse is true, and the lender benefits from repayment of a higher value of the same nominal amount. A key note, however, is that since the U.S. federal government is the largest debt holder in the global economy, there is a tendency toward higher inflation. Further, if inflation is uncertain, there may be reticence to engage in loans or other longer term transactions, which can cause corporate stagnation, an obviously important point for companies seeking to use leverage (debt) in their operations.

Key points:

- Inflation is the rise of prices associated with an increase in money supply at a faster rate than demand.
- Central banks may attempt to control inflation by modifying the currency supply.
- Higher inflation results in the ability to pay back liabilities with lower value currency (effectively decreasing the interest rate); the converse is also true, where lower inflation results in payback of liabilities at an effectively higher interest rate.

Hyperinflation

Hyperinflation is a term used when inflation rates exceed 50%. This is typically caused by rapid growth of the supply of paper money. The best studied example is post-WWI Germany, where the Weimar Republic was faced with having to pay reparations from the war, as well as stimulating economic growth. By increasing the money supply, the government was attempting to broach both issues. Not unexpectedly, there was a loss of confidence in the worth of the currency, thus removing any ability for supply and demand to reach equilibrium. Indeed, the *monthly* inflation rate was >300% – it was estimated that gas prices *quadrupled* every month during this time! Only by introducing a fixed value currency (the Rentenmark), which could be exchanged for a bond with a specific gold value, did confidence return into German currency, with subsequent stabilization of prices.

ADDITIONAL READING

Gerlach, P., Hordahl, P., Moessner, R., 2011. Inflation expectations and the great recession. BIS Quarterly Review, March, 39–51.

Mills, G.T., 1996. The impact of inflation on capital budgeting and working capital. Journal Of Financial And Strategic Decisions 9, 79–87.

CPI Inflation Calculator, Bureau of Labor Statistics, <http://www.bls.gov/data/inflation_calculator.htm>. (accessed 17 August 2012)

EXCHANGE RATES

Measuring Exchange Rates

Exchange rates are one of the most important concepts for technical executives to understand, particularly for those executives who deal with international transactions (sourcing, labor, commercialization, etc.). Nominal exchange rates relate to the price of one country's currency expressed in another country's currency, *viz.* it is the rate at which a country's currency can be exchanged for another's at a specific point in time. Indeed, these exchange rates change on a regular basis, and can be measured or expressed in different ways. A *"spot" exchange rate* is that which exists for a currency at current market prices; it changes on a minute-to-minute basis, related to the flow of supply and demand for a currency. An *"effective" exchange rate* is a weighted index of value against a basket of international currencies, where weighting is related to the portion or ratio of trade between countries (see also "Purchase Power Parity", below). The *"forward" exchange rate* involves the delivery of a currency at a given rate at some time in the future; it is a hedge against changes in exchange rate uncertainty. *"Bilateral" exchange rates* compare one currency directly with another (e.g., dollar/yen), and the *"real" exchange rate* is the ratio of domestic price indices between two countries. Within a given company, it is often the case that when executives discuss exchange rates, they are referring to either the spot or a bilateral rate, since the goods and services are being evaluated relative to a specific country.

Key points:

• Exchange rates are the value of one currency expressed in another's currency.

• While there are several different ways to measure exchange rates, the spot and the bilateral exchange rates are the most commonly used for company purposes.

Exchange Rate Systems

In addition to the exchange rate measurement, the technical executive should be aware that there are several *exchange rate systems* that affect the purchase of materials, goods, and services. Each tends to be used for different purposes by countries, usually with the goal of stabilizing the respective currencies in a global economy. In general, the two extremes in the systems of exchange rates are the *free floating exchange rate* and the *fixed exchange rate*. In the *free floating exchange rate, the value of a currency is explicitly related to the demand for the currency and its respective supply.* As a result, the trade of goods and services between countries influences this rate; there is no intervention by a central bank. While, as a pure play, this is an uncommon system for currency exchange, the notable exception existing within this paradigm is the United Kingdom, which has had a free floating exchange rate for the pound sterling since the 1990s. One advantage of floating exchange rates is a reduced need for foreign currency reserves by the central bank (there is no "target" exchange rate); additionally, it allows for "self-correction" with a significant trade deficit (decreases exchange rate, and makes goods from the country relatively less expensive domestically and abroad), and similarly, allows for growth with increased export demand (see also the "Purchasing Power Parity" section later in this chapter.). Nonetheless, altering interest rates *will* affect the exchange rate, so a central bank as needed may opt to alter foreign exchange by this mechanism as well (see below).

In contrast, a *fixed exchange rate is based on a country's government stipulating a specific rate based on "pegging" (assigning) the value of their currency to another item —* either a currency (e.g., U.S. dollar) or precious metals (e.g., gold). Because the exchange rate is pegged, there is no fluctuation from the established central rate, and there is consistency regarding costs; thus, competitiveness can improve with reductions in costs since the exchange rates will be stable. Other advantages in fixed rates include lower currency risk, and thus limited need to hedge in forward exchange rate markets (see above), and stimulation of certain levels of competitiveness, where domestic producers need to keep costs under control to maintain their competitive advantage with respect to price, and countries abroad need higher productivity to be able to compete with domestic companies. China held a fixed exchange rate pegged against the U.S. dollar until 1995, when they changed systems and allowed their currency to move against a basket of currencies (but still primarily influenced by the dollar).

Two other exchange rate systems exist that are in between the free floating and the fixed exchange rate systems. The *managed floating exchange rate system involves both market demand and involvement of the central bank.* While the value of the currency is based on supply and demand in the market, the central bank keeps a wary eye on the exchange rate, and acts as a buffer to prevent large changes over relatively short periods of time, typically daily. This is one of the more common systems present today, allowing for central bank flexibility to at least a modicum of situations (e.g. trade and inflation). While this approach is more closely aligned with a free floating rate, the *semi-fixed exchange rate* is more like a fixed exchange rate. The *semi-fixed exchange rate system still uses a specific target, but the actual exchange rate may move between a defined range on a day-to-day basis*; the central bank's role is to ensure that the exchange rate is within the given range by buying or selling currency as appropriate.

Key points:

- Free floating exchange rates relate to the demand and the supply of a currency, with no intervention by the central bank.
- Fixed exchange rates are based on a specific target, typically pegged to another country's currency.
- Managed floating exchange rates allow floating of the rate based on supply and demand but also allow intervention to avoid significant fluctuations in value.
- Semi-fixed exchange rates target a given rate, but allow fluctuations in a range, which is maintained by the central bank's buying and selling of currency.

ADDITIONAL READING

Sarno, L., Taylor, M.P., 2002. The Economics of Exchange Rates. Cambridge University Press, New York.
Foreign Exchange Rates, Federal Bank of New York, <http://www.ny.frb.org/markets/fxrates/noon.cfm>. (accessed 17 August 2012)
FXStreet.com, <http://www.fxstreet.com>. (accessed 18 August 2012)

Purchasing Power Parity

Purchasing power parity relates to a presumed equilibrium between exchange rates, based on price; without barriers to trade, *the assumption is that identical goods will have the same price in different markets.* For a given item, if the price in one country increases, then the demand for the currency *of that country* will decrease in the other country, and thus, *the exchange rate will adjust* until the relative price is the same once again for both countries for the good in question. In practice, purchasing power parity is assessed for a "basket of goods" (although there are similar comparisons with single items, such as the "Big Mac Index," or the "Starbucks Tall Latte Index"). Indeed, there are usually significant differences between nominal exchange rates and the purchasing power parity rate; an often cited example is that in 2003, the GDP *per capita* in India was about US$1,700 based on nominal exchange rates, while it was US$3,600 based on a purchasing power parity evaluation. This obviously has significant implications for company strategy with respect to a variety of aspects, from locating facilities in certain countries, to wages and benefits to be paid employees, as well as overall costs.

Another key aspect of purchasing power parity involves the understanding that the nominal exchange rate and the purchasing power parity rate best represent certain types of goods and services. *Tradable, nonperishable goods tend to trade nearer to the nominal exchange rate, while local nontradable goods and services fall closer to the purchasing power parity rates.* Hence, the implication is that there exists a sustainable cost advantage to produce tradable items in low income countries, not only because the worker cost is lower, but also because their pay goes further than in higher income countries. Further, for nontradable goods closer to the purchasing power parity rates, a cost advantage occurs with local plants, since while the product price is closer to purchasing power exchange rates, they can be paid for by cheaper nominal exchange rates, which would not be possible in richer countries. Of note is that *any transport costs or governmental intervention weakens purchasing power parity*, since such costs diminish the relationship between exchange rates and the assumption that identical goods will have the same price in different markets.

Key points:

- Purchase power parity is a concept where the price of a product or service is the same (assuming no trade barriers) in different markets, and the exchange rate adjusts to ensure equivalence.
- The nominal exchange rate and the purchase power parity rate are not the same.
- Tradable goods are more closely aligned with nominal exchange rates, while nontradable goods and services more closely align with purchasing power parity rates.

ADDITIONAL READING

Taylor, A.M., 2002. A century of purchasing-power parity. Rev. Econ. Stat. 84, 139–150.

Ong, L.L., 2003. The Big Mac Index: Applications of Purchasing Power Parity. Palgrave MacMilan, New York.

Organization for Economic Co-operation and Development, Monthly Comparative Price Levels (Purchasing Power Parity), <http://stats.oecd.org/Index.aspx?DataSetCode = CPL>. (accessed 16 August 2012)

Governmental Role and Implications of Exchange Rate Changes

As noted, while governments (*viz.* central banks) can utilize exchange rate systems to modify the supply and demand of currency and thereby the nominal exchange rate, they can also indirectly affect exchange rates in other ways. Already mentioned are government policies for modifying free transport of goods across international borders, which affect both purchasing power parity as well as nominal exchange rates. However, alterations in the level of currency in circulation (and ultimately, influencing interest rates) also modifies exchange rates, as do purchases of other currencies based on supply and demand as noted previously. Further, with interest rate changes due to changes in governmental policy (e.g., response to inflation), currency may be exchanged for the most favorable return by foreign exchange traders. Hence, any governmental policy that increases the demand for a specific currency will result in an increase in nominal exchange rates in foreign exchange markets, with the converse also being true.

Clearly, the changes in exchange rates result in differences in both demand and remuneration received by the firm. When the domestic currency (e.g., dollar) is strong, importers must pay more to buy the products of the firm, and thus, the overall demand for the product is less; it also decreases domestic prices (since the value of the domestic currency is higher), further exacerbating value capture by the company. Of course, if the supply or value chain includes materials from abroad, the overall costs could be less due to the higher value of the currency and its relative ability to buy more. In contrast, with a weaker domestic currency, there is a decreased price of domestically produced products and services abroad, and thus an increase in demand. Such increased demand in foreign countries results in an increase in prices domestically, as well as an increase in profitability. Moreover, because foreign currency is more valuable, prices of imports increase, resulting in a decrease in demand for such products. Again, as noted, this can have an impact on the company if materials for products are sourced abroad. At the very extreme, sharp declines in value of a domestic currency like the dollar could result in a response by the central bank to increase interest rates to mitigate the potential for inflation; as such, the cost of capital (see Chapter 6 on finance) would increase which would have potential detrimental effects on projects or programs being considered within the firm. Also, there is a direct effect between exchange rate changes and inflation; with alterations in exchange rate, the CPI is affected directly, with resultant movement of demand as described previously. There is thus an inextricable tie between the exchange rate and the relative inflationary pressure it may cause, and which central banks need to consider when formulating policy (which will affect businesses in domestic and foreign entities).

Key points:

- Governments can influence exchange rates directly and indirectly by policy changes and altering the levels of currency in circulation.
- Strong domestic currency decreases demand abroad and makes imports cheaper, thereby increasing demand of such imports; weak domestic currency increases demand in foreign countries, making imports more expensive and thus decreasing demand for imports.
- Considerations of foreign sourcing (and sales) are directly affected by exchange rates.
- Exchange rates and inflation are tied together in that changes in one will alter the other.

ADDITIONAL READING

Alfaro, L., Di Tella, R., 2008. China: To Float or Not to Float. HBS No. 9-706-021. Harvard Business School Publishing, Boston.

Kenen, P.B., 2000. Fixed v. floating exchange rates. Cato Journal 20, 109–113.

Priyo, A.K.K., 2009. Impact of the exchange rate regime change on the value of Bangladesh currency. Soc. Sci. Rev. 26 (1), 185–214.

INNOVATION AND ECONOMICS

Innovation represents a significant influence on economics (and *vice versa*). Indeed, innovation not only spurs economic growth, but is fundamental both on a microeconomic as well as macroeconomic scale. Industries and firms often compete on a microeconomic level, and with globalization, must also consider macroeconomic factors. In addition, countries must compete with each other not only for the outputs of productivity, but also for the industries and firms that will generate the inputs. Hence, the interplay of economics and innovation revolves around facilitating higher productivity *via* innovation by using economic policy, and economic growth is driven by innovative capacity derived from knowledge and technology.

Joseph Schumpeter, an economist writing in the 20th century, provided the structural underpinnings of the relationship between innovation and economics. Economic functions in the Schumpeterian paradigm included invention (the development of a new idea), innovation (product development and commercialization) and diffusion (imitation by competitors); of these, innovation was the most relevant in economic development, according to Schumpeter, because of a direct relationship to commercialization. Hence, because entrepreneurs were the drivers of innovation, they play a particularly important role in the process.

An extension and quantification of this relationship of innovation to economic growth was described by Moses Abramowitz. To increase the outputs of an economy, one can either increase the inputs into production (so-called "factor growth") or one can develop ways to increase output given the same inputs. By examining the growth of outputs in the U.S. from 1870 to 1950, he found that factor growth only accounted for about 15% of the growth of outputs of the economy. Robert Solow found similar data when examining other time periods; these data have been seen not only in the U.S., but in other country's economies as well (e.g., East Asia). Indeed, it is *technology development* that accounts for the increasing productivity of outputs, manifest as innovation. Note that these developments include not only new technologies, but also incremental improvements to existing products. Further, the technological developments not only spawn from the industries in which the inventions were derived, but also and importantly from the creativity of the users who innovated these products over time (well documented by von Hippel, 2005). While inventors may have conceptualized the usage of given ideas for particular purposes, it is clear that other innovative users have been able to take these technologies and push use them in ways far beyond what was originally conceived (see the box on the next page entitled "Clusters"). Schumpeter conceptualized the term "creative destruction" to describe the replacement of innovations, where new innovations replace old ones (and the inherent firms, infrastructure, and profits around them) as the cycle of invention, innovation, and imitation occurs. User innovation can extend this cycle, prolonging and modifying creative destruction by user influenced changes in the life cycle, for the benefit of firms, industries, and countries involved in the production of these products. Technical executives need to recognize the macro- and microeconomic policies that support innovation, from the perspective of outputs from firms, to enhancing a milieu of user innovation as inputs for the R&D process.

Key points:
- Innovation and economics are integrally related and account for significant levels of productivity outputs.
- According to Schumpeterian economics, innovation represents the most important factor in economic growth and development.
- User-based innovation is an important aspect that can modify products developed for other uses and prolong the "creative destruction" cycle.

Clusters

Governments can play key roles in innovation, particularly through economic policies and supportive activities. It is axiomatic that a country's economy is based on the collection of companies and industries located there – the success of these companies will fuel the development of the country's economy. Hence, providing incentives and infrastructure can be key in successfully navigating the waters of competition and providing an environment in which innovation is fostered. An example of such a set of policies includes the geographic construction of "clusters," where governments set up and encourage regions of similar technologies to spur innovation. Providing matching incentives on both the supply side (e.g., capital, labor, production, communications, etc.) as well as the demand side (e.g., consumers, services, infrastructure) drives the innovative process. Areas such as Silicon Valley, CA (for information technology), Hyderabad, India and Sorrento Valley (San Diego), CA (for biotechnology), Cambridge, MA (for nanotechnology), and Rio de Janeiro, Brazil (for petrochemical engineering) are examples of clusters where high levels of innovation occur.

Bresnahan T., Gambardella A. (2004) Building High-Tech Clusters: Silicon Valley and Beyond. Cambridge: Cambridge University Press.

ADDITIONAL READING

Comin, D, Hobijn, B., 2010. An exploration of technology diffusion. Am. Econ. Rev. 100, 2031–2059.

Hall, B.H., Rosenberg, N. (Eds.), 2010. Handbook of Economics of Innovation. Elsevier, New York.

Von Hippel, E., 2005. Democratizing Innovation. MIT Press, Cambridge.

GENERAL REFERENCES AND WEBSITES IN ECONOMICS

Heilbroner, R., Milberg, W., 1998. The Making of Economic Society. Prentice Hall, Saddle River, NJ.

Moss, D.A., 2007. A Concise Guide to Macroeconomics: What Managers, Executives and Students Need to Know. Harvard Business School Press, Boston.

The Economist Magazine Website, <http://www.economist.com/>. (accessed 17 August 2012)

U.S. Bureau of Economic Analysis, <http://www.bea.gov/>. (accessed 15 August 2012)

Corporate Strategy

Table of Contents

> *"Strategy without tactics is the slowest route to victory. Tactics without strategy is the noise before defeat."*
>
> **Sun Tzu**

> *"You may not be interested in strategy, but strategy is interested in you."*
>
> **Leon Trotsky**

INTRODUCTION

While there are a myriad of definitions of strategy, a useful one for the technical executive is the reflection on and the execution of an approach to achieving business objectives. Indeed, objectives represent the overarching goals of the company; strategy is the approach by which such objectives and goals can be achieved. From a corporate perspective, strategy reflects the businesses and approaches senior managers have determined the company will complete; this will typically include the customers and products the firm will target to create value. Within that context, there are other strategies as well, which translate from the corporate strategies to the individual units within the company, from the earliest aspect of the value chain in R&D to products being commercialized. Hence, there can be an HR strategy, a marketing strategy, a manufacturing strategy, etc.; in an ideal world, each of these strategies will translate directly from the corporate strategy, which will in turn derive from the company objectives and goals.

There have been a number of paradigms used to articulate strategy for the firm, with different areas of emphasis. While each utilizes a different

The Pragmatic MBA for Scientific and Technical Executives
DOI: http://dx.doi.org/10.1016/B978-0-12-397932-2.00003-X

conceptual framework, they are all essentially complementary in their approaches in order to create an understanding on how to compete in the marketplace. It is important for technical executives to understand both the key concepts and vocabulary of the strategic imperatives and models in order to best formulate their own strategies for programs, products, and innovative approaches to perceived unmet needs; in this way, the technical executive becomes a more integrated part of the strategic team, and can better contribute to the ongoing success of the organization. Excellent reviews on strategy can be found in the references, particularly Chapter 1 of Collis and Montgomery, **Corporate Strategy: Resources and the Scope of the Firm** (1997) and Chapter 11, Hax, **The Delta Model** (2010).

While there are many examples of corporate strategy in use, four models have penetrated into corporations; their lexicons have spread throughout many senior management groups and technical teams would be well advised to be familiar with them. These include the *Business Portfolio Model*, from the Boston Consulting Group (BCG), the *Five Forces Model*, developed by Michael Porter, the *Resource-Based View*, by Birgner Wernerfelt, and the *Delta Model*, from Arnoldo Hax. Each of these models will be described in turn.

BUSINESS PORTFOLIO MODEL

This model of strategy assumes that a firm is a combination of different businesses (i.e., business units), and was developed in the late 1960s by Bruce Henderson, founder of BCG. As such, each unit is distinct from any other through its unique product–market economics, with the company being a *portfolio* of businesses where different internal and external environments exist. This results in a difference in relative competitive position as well as growth rate for each product group, which are considered the most relevant factors in determining a strategy for the individual business unit. These two factors interact, since the competitiveness of a business unit will determine the rate at which it will generate revenues, while the growth rate will influence how readily market share can be gained and the relative amount of value to be generated with additional resource allocation. This results in both a division of businesses into distinct categories ("matrix"), and the resultant strategies that can address such positioning. The Business Portfolio Model has been the basis for a number of other

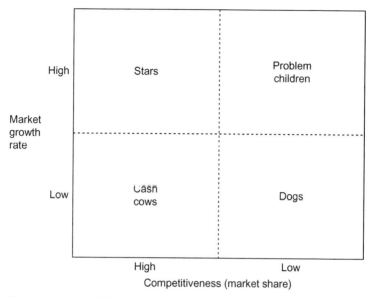

Figure 3.1 *Business Portfolio Matrix. Adapted from Boston Consulting Group, Perspectives on Experience. Boston: The Boston Consulting Group, 1974.*

matrix models extending upon and modifying components for comparison and integration.

Fundamentally, there are four existing categories based on business growth rate and competitive position ("market share"): *cash cows, stars, problem children*, and *dogs* (see Figure 3.1). *Cash cows* are those products where high market share exists, with low growth, and they represent more mature markets where relatively fewer resources are required to support the unit; these products/units generate more revenue in excess of that required to maintain market share. *Stars* are those business units whose products have high growth rate and high market share; these products generate (and use) significant amounts of resources and are typically at an earlier stage in the product life cycle (see Chapter 1 on Marketing). In contrast, units where there is low market share and high growth rates are considered *problem children*, as they require high levels of resources as a result of growth, but low market share results in low revenue generation; it is typical that these units require more resources than they generate. Finally, *dogs* are those units that have products of low competitive position and low business growth rate, and may occur late in a product life cycle; any revenues these products may

Table 3.1 Examples of Strategic Alternatives within the Business Portfolio Matrix

Business Unit/Product	Examples of Strategic Alternatives
Cash Cows	Diversification (within or outside current market within same segment)
	Joint Venture
Stars	Market Development and/or Penetration
	Integration/Consolidation
	Diversification (within market)
Problem Children	Market Development and/or Penetration
	Consolidation
	Divestment/Liquidation
Dogs	Liquidation
	Retrenchment

generate are consumed by the resources required to maintain market share; these products can drain resources from other more profitable segments, and represent significant opportunity cost for a company.

By defining where a particular business unit falls within the model, one can conceptually identify the appropriate strategy to utilize for that particular product or products. As an example, a firm with stars that have high growth and strong competitive positioning may utilize a strategy to focus on the current products to ensure maximum penetration, or acquire new products similar to that of the star (concentric diversification). Business units with cash cows may also benefit from diversification, while problem children, while having opportunities for growth, may benefit from either additional resource investment or examination on the lack of efficacy in capturing value. Finally, business units with dogs may require divestment, or potentially retrenchment if the exit costs are too high. Table 3.1 shows examples of strategic alternatives for each component of the matrix; additional readings provide more detail on these strategic alternatives.

Key points:

- The Business Portfolio Model is based on the two variables of market growth rate and competitive positioning (market share).
- Companies consist of products/business units which can be classified into a matrix, as a function of these component variables (cash cows, stars, problem children, dogs).
- Classification allows for the choice of particular strategies that are appropriate for that type of product/unit.

Strategy: The Course of Evolutionary Biology

Bruce Henderson, the inventor of the BCG Matrix, articulated the important similarities (and differences) between strategy and evolution. Because evolutionary biology is related to one of the greatest insights of biological systems, *viz.* survival of the fittest, it is not surprising that analogies can be drawn between the two. Indeed, Darwin noted, in the seminal text **On the Origin of Species**, the importance of adaptability to change as a key component of competitive advantage. While in biological systems this is related to genetic and phenotypic diversity, with natural selection taking place over many generations, in business, strategy (i.e., choice in resource allocation and direction) foists a given "phenotype" on a business or unit, and hence a proposed competitive advantage. If this choice of strategy differentiates the business well enough from and allows the business to adapt better to the environment than competitors, it will survive; if not, it will fail – as would any species that did not have evolutionarily advantaged traits in a given environment. Instead of taking generations to play out, the business evolutionary competition manifest itself within market cycles.

Henderson BD. The Origin of Strategy (1989), Harvard Business Review, Nov–Dec.

ADDITIONAL READING

Ionescu, F.L., 2011. Boston Consulting Group II – a business portfolio analysis matrix. International Journal of Economic Practices and Theories, 1, 2247–7225.

Morrison, A., Wensley, R., 1991. Boxing up or boxed in? A short history of the Boston Consulting Group share/growth matrix. Journal of Marketing Management 7, 105–129.

Stern, C.W., Stalk Jr., G. (Eds.), 1998. Perspectives on Strategy from the Boston Consulting Group. John Wiley & Sons, New York.

FIVE FORCES MODEL

Arguably the most influential model of corporate strategy today is the Five Forces Model, articulated in the 1980s by Michael Porter of the Harvard Business School. This model has developed a unique framework and vocabulary for the formulation of corporate strategy since its initial description, and focuses on *competitive positioning* and *industry structure*. This model is based on an "attractive industry" where profitability can be achieved based on the "five forces" (bargaining power of suppliers, bargaining power of buyers, threat of new entrants, threat of substitutes, and rivalry

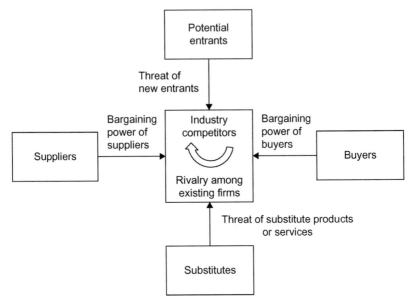

Figure 3.2 *Five Forces Model: Forces Driving Industry Competition. Adapted from M.E. Porter, Competitive Strategy: Techniques for Analyzing Industries and Competitors. New York: The Free Press, 1980.*

within the industry), which impact competitiveness (Figure 3.2), wherein competitive positioning allows for sustaining competitive advantage.

Indeed, the Five Forces drive the profit *potential* of an industry, by influencing the prices, costs, and needed resources for the business. By identifying the strength of the Five Forces, one can determine the relative attractiveness of the business (or not!) for entry. In this model, a firm (only) competes effectively in an attractive industry on the basis of either *low cost* or *differentiation*. This is a result of the efficiency of low-cost companies' cost structures, which allows pricing below others within the industry; in contrast, firms may compete on the basis of differentiation, where unique product attributes attract buyers and allow for a price premium to be paid. Hence, despite the articulation of the product differentiation versus low cost concept, the Five Forces Model emphasizes the nature of the industry, rather than the product *per se* (as does the BCG Model). Moreover, these activities are based on an internal "value chain" (Figure 3.3) that executes the positioning within the industry. These include *primary* activities (inbound logistics, operations, outbound logistics, marketing and sales, and service) and *support* activities (firm infrastructure,

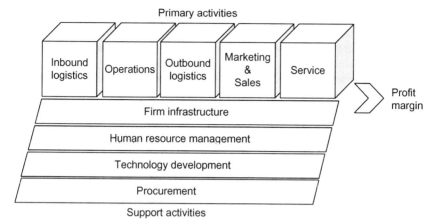

Figure 3.3 *Five Forces Value Chain. Adapted from M.E. Porter, Competitive Strategy: Techninques for Analyzing Industries and Competitors. New York: The Free Press, 1980.*

human resources, technology development, and procurement). Each of these activities are linked, depending on the industry or type of competitive advantage addressed; primary activities can be linked with either primary or support activities. In either case, such activities must be performed in an efficient manner allowing a customer to derive more value than the costs to deliver the product or service (*viz.* generation of a profit margin). The value chain is the opportunity of the firm to create value, and indeed, Porter articulates arguments that show how the configuration of the value chain (and *re*configuration of the value chain, as necessary) by companies allows for the achievement of competitive advantage. The choices made on controlling the *drivers* of the value chain can create an advantage based on differentiation or low cost competitiveness. Hence, the Five Forces Model is based on achieving competitive advantage, by picking an attractive industry and achieving low cost or differentiation through unique activities that generate an efficient value chain.

Key points:
- The Five Forces Model was the first to encompass a comprehensive paradigm of corporate strategy.
- The focus of the model is on an attractive industry and product positioning based on the five forces to which firms are subjected.
- The value chain consists of internal components of the firm to create products or services.
- Competitive advantage is based on either low cost or differentiation.

The Pharmaceutical Industry: Retaining Competitive Advantage

In the Five Forces Model, industries are a compilation of a variety of different players, including suppliers, buyers, potential new entrants, incumbents, and possible substitutes. Each of these individual players can garner competitive advantage, based on positioning itself in a limited number of facets, viz. cost leadership, differentiation, or focus within the market. An attractive industry, then, is one where one can gain and retain competitive advantage in the context of the five forces. The pharmaceutical industry fulfills many components of an attractive industry articulated in the Five Forces Model. Supplier power is low for most small molecule drugs; there is significant buying power in the pharmaceutical industry for chemicals, which are considered for the most part commodities (however, biological drugs are another matter; see the box "Quality Management: The Cost of Failure" in Chapter 8). The buyer, primarily consumers (patients), has little choice in what can be purchased – physicians are a key influencer of medications to be purchased by patients through their respective insurance plans. While there may be a choice between generic drug substitutes and "name brand" products, unless a patient is willing to take the time and effort to question or search out another provider for alternative medications, he or she has little choice if they require a given drug. There is a significant barrier to entry into the industry – this includes being able to negotiate the treacherous waters of an antiquated regulatory system that has not kept pace with the developments of the technological outputs of the pharmaceutical companies (and resultant R&D expertise built up in a variety of different areas) to the economics of scale in operation and manufacturing as well as sales and marketing needed to make a product successful. However, that being noted, the competition between incumbents is significant, with large capitalization companies going head-to head in competition with products to treat the exact same indications. Finally, as noted previously, the only "substitution" at the point of sale are generics; other competitive agents (e.g., from other manufacturers) are typically not a possibility as a substitute unless a patient is willing to ask for another medication, which requires very high levels of sophistication. Hence, given the limited power of suppliers, buyers, new entrants, and substitutes, and the ability to focus on a small number of incumbent firms, the pharmaceutical industry in the U.S. is a very attractive industry as described by the Five Forces Model.

ADDITIONAL READING

Karagiannopoulos, G.D., Georgopoulos, N., Nikolopoulos, K., 2005. Fathoming Porter's five forces model in the Internet era. info 7, 66–76.

Porter, M.E., 1980. Competitive Strategy: Techniques for Analyzing Industries and Competitors. Free Press, New York, NY.

RESOURCE-BASED VIEW OF THE FIRM

While the Five Forces Model is associated with picking an attractive industry and product positioning (low cost vs. differentiation), the Resource-Based View (RBV) focuses on the firm itself, and the "competencies" and "resources" required to compete effectively in the marketplace. This model was articulated formally by Birgner Wernerfelt, of the Sloan School of Management (MIT) in the mid-1980s (although components were described earlier), and expanded upon by a number of other groups [e.g., CK Prahalad and Gary Hamel of the Ross School of Business (University of Michigan) and Cynthia Montgomery and David Collis of Harvard Business School]. The paradigm of this model is the achievement and acquisition of the appropriate resources, allowing the firm to establish competitive advantage in the marketplace. Associated with this is the determination of *core competencies*, i.e., the combination of knowledge and/or technical capabilities allowing a business to be competitive in the marketplace; these are key resources the firm should strive to acquire or develop. As such, these resources can be classified in three main categories:

1. *Tangible Assets*: These may appear on the balance sheet of the firm. Such assets are typically relevant to the firm's strategy, but may not, *per se*, allow competitive advantage due to the standard nature of the asset. An example of this would be factories in a low cost region, which may be of value to the firm, but may not be of distinct advantage in and of themselves; contrast this to real estate next to a popular tourist site, which although a "standard" asset, could provide significant competitive advantage to a given firm.

2. *Intangible Assets*: Most often these assets do not appear on the balance sheet, and they play an important role in the firm's strategy; they are difficult to imitate, thus providing value to the company and competitive advantage. Examples of intangible assets are patents, trademarks, brand, and reputation.

3. *Organizational Capabilities*: These are complex combinations of assets, including people and processes. Examples include lean manufacturing and low cost structures. Such aspects are able to transform inputs into outputs, thereby creating value by meeting customer needs.

   In general, resources should have the following specific traits:

- *Valuable*: Resources must allow companies to execute a value-creating strategy, by outperforming competitors and/or reducing weaknesses.
- *Rare*: Resources must be rare, almost by definition, in the context of the noted categories.

- *Inimitable*: Resources controlled by very few (and preferably only one) firm(s) have the potential to be a source of a competitive advantage.
- *Nonsubstitutable*: Regardless if a resource is valuable, rare, and inimitable, if it is substitutable, it will not be relevant for competitive advantage.

Hence, RBV is about obtaining and developing resources and capabilities that form the basis of core competencies of the firm, and as such, by preventing imitation or substitution (by competitors) the firm maintains its competitive advantage.

Key points:

- In the RBV Model, the focus is on the firm and the development of appropriate resources.
- It is the acquisition and preservation of assets and capabilities that is the primary function of the firm.
- Competitive advantage is based on achievement and deployment of unique resources and capabilities.
- The prevention of either substitution or imitation of resources and capabilities allows companies to sustain their competitive advantage.

Creating Resources: Southwest Airlines

The Resource-Based View of the firm emphasizes that competitive advantage is a manifestation of the internal resources and capabilities generated or acquired by the firm. These collections of resources and capabilities create a milieu which the firm occupies in the marketplace, particularly if structured in a way which is unique. Probably one of the best studied examples of the development of unique resources is the Southwest Airlines model. Despite operating in a challenging industry, where much of the operational components are "common" and commoditized, Southwest has build a formidable company by combining resources in such a way that imitation is difficult and competitive advantage is high; indeed, Southwest's market cap is larger than the combined market cap of its six competitors. Southwest has built resources and capabilities based on simplicity, low cost, and the understanding that only planes in the air generate value. Every component of Southwest targets minimizing turnaround time: by combining use of only one type of plane (Boeing 737) (allows easier service), no meals (no requirements to "reload" service areas), flying into uncongested airports (allowing easier transitions and air traffic control routings), no assigned seats (encouraging passengers to arrive early to airports) and, more recently, "bags fly free" (minimizing the time required to board and stow carry-ons), Southwest has increased its ability to keep planes in the air, thereby generating more revenue by transporting more passengers. Moreover, the lack of a hub and spoke system also minimizes time spent at the gate; these point-to-point routes and gate privileges at less congested airports are key resources that are difficult to emulate given the structure of competing airlines. Thus, combined with an internal culture of positivity, entrepreneurship, and team orientation, Southwest has produced a unique compilation of resources, which has often been emulated but is difficult to match.

ADDITIONAL READING

Collis, D.J., Montgomery, C.A., 1997. Corporate Strategy: Resources and the Scope of the Firm. Irwin McGraw-Hill, New York.

Conner, K.R., Prahalad, C.K., 1996. A resource-based theory of the firm: knowledge versus opportunism. Organization Science 7, 477–501.

Prahalad, C.K., Hamel, G., 1990, May–June. The core competencies of the corporation. Harv. Bus. Rev., 79–91.

Wernerfelt, B., 1984. A resource-based view of the firm. Strateg. Manage. J. 5, 171–180.

DELTA MODEL

The Delta Model was initially developed by Arnoldo Hax and colleagues from the Sloan School of Management (MIT) in the late 1990s. This model is unique in that, in addition to taking into account the industry, products, and firm, there is an emphasis on the *customer* and *cooperation* in the marketplace, rather than rivalry to generate competitive advantage. In particular, there is an emphasis on *customer segmentation* and derived capabilities of the company, which then define the mission and strategic agenda of the firm. The firm emphasis of this model of strategy is that the center of strategy is the customer, and the goal is *customer bonding* wherein a mutually beneficial relationship is created. The model also emphasizes both *service* components and *complementors* (those firms that are *part of the value chain* of providing for customer needs by the firm) generating an *extended enterprise* to create opportunity for value for the firm (and customers). The three main strategic positions include:

1. Best product positioning (either by low cost or differentiation)
2. Total customer solution (satisfying both product and service needs)
3. System lock-in (essentially a monopolistic position)

   In between each of these major positions are more blended positions encompassing additional components, which generally more deeply

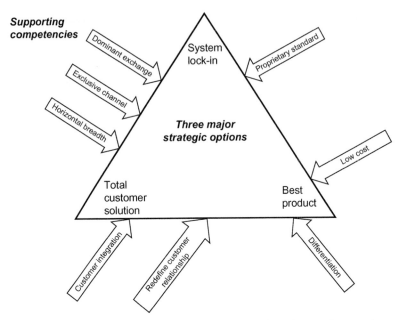

Figure 3.4 *The Delta Model.* *There are three main strategic options and supporting competencies; these allow customer segmentation and assignment of capabilities. Adapted from A.C. Hax, The Delta Model: Reinventing Your Business Strategy. New York: Springer, 2010.*

support the relationship with the customer. As noted, customer segmentation is key in the development of strategy for the firm (Figure 3.4), and is the initial consideration in any subsequent development.

Further, these customer segmentations identify potential opportunities for the company, based on different aspects of the customer characteristics and capabilities present or being developed by the firm, and the *value proposition* the firm can therefore offer the customer. These capabilities are identified utilizing the firm's previously identified competencies. By being able to match such capabilities with customer needs, the model allows for the generation of a strategic agenda and monitoring systems (including budgets addressing both short and long term strategic agendas, as well as the customer, organizational learning, and business perspectives) allowing for the measure of successful implementation of the strategy (Figure 3.5). The Delta Model thus encompasses the Business Portfolio Model, assessing the dynamics of product characteristics, the Five Forces Model, in the focus on

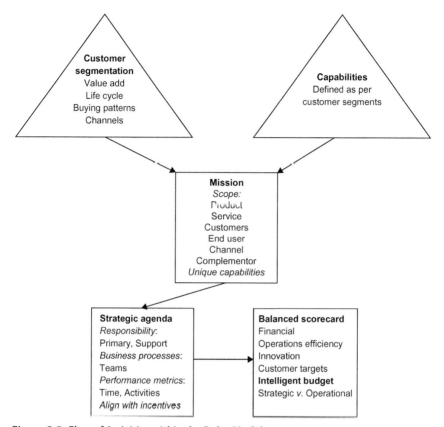

Figure 3.5 *Flow of Activities within the Delta Model.*

the nature of the product and industry (recall competition is based on low cost or differentiation), and the RBV Model (based on internal resources and capabilities of the firm to provide competitive advantage).

Key points:

- Companies should focus on the customer as the center of strategic positioning rather than only the industry or firm.
- Building an extended enterprise of products and service offerings to address total customer solutions represents the most effective way to compete (cooperation rather than competition).
- Strategy is built one customer at a time from a granular understanding of needs/wants manifest by where the customer sits within a respective customer segmentation.

Strategy for the Not-for-Profit

The Delta Model encompasses customer segmentation as the prime consideration for the development of strategy. This strategy eschews imitation and focuses on a deep understanding of the customer by producing a value proposition that is differentiated and unique. Moreover, strategy revolves around a myriad of stakeholders, i.e., the extended enterprise (consisting of the entire value chain of suppliers, customers, and providers). As noted, there are eight competencies within the model (low cost, differentiation, redefining the customer relationship, customer integration, horizontal breadth, restricted access, dominant exchange, and proprietary standard) around the fundamental strategic positions of system lock-in, total customer solution, and best product positioning. Perhaps in contrast to other articulations of strategy, the Delta Model has also been conceptualized to encompass not-for-profit organizations (defined as those whose objective is social benefit rather than a specific profit motive). Indeed, by *redefining the customer* as those who both contribute to the organization as well as those who benefit from it, the Delta Model can be used to segment stakeholders to be served and value propositions to be offered. In this case, the customer segmentation is somewhat modified in terminology, as noted in the table on the following page, with different value propositions. In addition, many not-for-profit organizations have a unique positioning at system lock- (as opposed to for-profit businesses, which often start at best product), not as a result of competing, but rather because of a lack of competition; as a result, not-for-profits ought to move towards *best product strategy* first, to enhance efficiencies in infrastructure and develop differentiated products; it is only after gaining these efficiencies that an organization can then proceed toward a total customer solution strategy, where customized solutions can take place. Hence, by understanding the customer segmentation particular to a specific not-for-profit firm the Delta Model allows for a cogent and comprehensive approach to defining a strategy for serving "customers" in the not-for-profit world.

Sidebar Table: Strategy for the Not-for-Profit

Business Strategy	Redefined for Not-For-Profit	Not-For-Profit Strategic Example
Low cost	Administrative efficiency	Bush–Clinton Katrina fund: 100% of contributions to be used for grants
Differentiation	Differentiation	Bill & Melinda Gates Foundation: focus on (amongst other things) prevention of infectious diseases in underserved populations
Redefining customer relationship	Attraction/ development of customer	Public Broadcasting System fund raisers: offers access to special events, including live shows and recording of popular programs; hosted events by local celebrities and experts on interesting subjects
Customer integration	Knowledge transferred	Universities: business of education
Horizontal breadth	Total breadth of offering	British Library: houses and makes available its entire offerings including PhD theses written in the UK
Restricted access	Channels of delivery	Doctors without Borders: are allowed unique access to sensitive political areas of the world for humanitarian efforts
Dominant exchange	System support	National Institutes of Health: provides information and infrastructure support for funding of biomedical and related research subjects
Proprietary standard	Intellectual value	Genbank: depository of unique sequences (and tools) for use in biologic and related research

Hax, A., 2010. The Delta Model. Springer, New York.

Table 3.2 compares the strategic components described. As noted, each of these approaches are complementary, although activities to address the marketplace are different. The technical executive should have familiarity with each of these popular approaches as they have different components that will directly impact both early R&D as well as support of the commercial organization from the technical staff.

Table 3.2 Comparison of Strategic Approaches

	BCG Business Portfolio Model	Five Forces Model	Resource-Based View	Delta Model
Scope	Business (Unit) portfolio	Industry	Firm as a whole	Firm and complementors
Techniques of Analysis	Product characterization based on market growth and share	Determination of ability to compete on low cost or differentiation	Evaluation of resource requirements (tangible, intangible, organizational capabilities)	Customer segmentation and capabilities assessment
Strategic Intent	Product/unit characteristics dictate strategy	Competitive positioning in attractive industry	Acquisition of appropriate resources	Development of an extended enterprise
Tactical Goals	Market share	Product economics	Development of core competencies	Customer bonding

ADDITIONAL READING

Hax, A., 2010. The Delta Model. Springer, New York.

Jutla, D.N., Yu, W., 2008. Applying the delta model to mobile marketing management in the US marketplace. International Journal of Electronic Business 6, 216–231.

GENERAL REFERENCES AND WEBSITES IN STRATEGY

Barney, J.B., 1986. Strategic factor markets: expectations, luck and business strategy. Manag. Sci. 32, 1231–1241.

Mansfield, G.M., Fourie, L.C.H., 2004. Strategy and business models – strange bedfellows? A case for convergence and its evolution into strategic architecture. South African Journal of Business Management 35, 35–44.

Stewart, M., 2009. The Management Myth: Why the Experts Keep Getting It Wrong. W.W. Norton and Company, New York.

Thompson, A.A., Strickland, A.J., 1981. Strategy and Policy Concepts and Cases. Business Publications, Inc., Dallas.

Business Strategy Review Magazine, <http://bsr.london.edu/home/index.html>. (accessed 17 August 2012)

CHAPTER 4

Management and Leadership

Table of Contents

> *"If I have seen farther than others, it is because I was standing on the shoulders of giants."*
>
> **Isaac Newton**

> *"The leadership instinct you are born with is the backbone. You develop the funny bone and the wishbone that go with it."*
>
> **Elaine Agather**

INTRODUCTION

Arguably, a primary responsibility of the technical executive is to manage innovation and the innovation process. Within this context, not only is a fundamental understanding of science required, but also a knowledge of the unique requirements that underpin the motivation of technical professionals and personnel. Indeed, there are a myriad of publications identifying the unique aspects of this group, and thus the managerial and leadership challenges inherent in a technical organization. Moreover, in many highly specialized industries, the types of structure within an organizational framework have significant implications. Because of the unusual degree of technical expertise required in these organizations, the need for

The Pragmatic MBA for Scientific and Technical Executives
DOI: http://dx.doi.org/10.1016/B978-0-12-397932-2.00004-1

multifunctional product development teams arise; in the structure of such teams, there are clearly advantages and disadvantages to a particular structure, delineated by several factors of which the technical executive should be aware. Understanding the advantages of team structures and the unique aspects of managing technical personnel will allow the R&D executive better clarity on approaches that may be useful for maximizing productivity in the organization.

TEAM STRUCTURE

Fundamentally, innovation is the ability to see the usefulness of an invention along with the ability to capitalize on this realization by development. Capitalization by development requires a level of communication (often in a myriad of different ways) that may be executed by the formation of teams. Hence, the innovation process may be *managed* by facilitating communication (and thus the transfer of knowledge), manifest by the formation of teams that consist of members with diverse areas of expertise who can together develop the necessary technology.

Several studies have shown that teams best function by evaluating response to (1) technology development and (2) the marketplace. These two activities can be thought of as an "inward" and "outward" view from the perspective of the firm. Both are relevant to the innovation process, as the first contemplates the capabilities of the company, and the second revolves around the needs of the marketplace into which the company (whether directly or indirectly) sells. Nonetheless, a lateral (*cf.* hierarchical) structure of the technical team has been found to have significant value, primarily due to the need for collaboration amongst technical staff with differing areas of expertise.

Departmental Teams: Addressing Technology

An organization can arrange its teams to specifically address technology development, which most often is represented by teams that are within a departmental, specialized structure. In this case, the team members reflect similar backgrounds, and there is close proximity between technical experts within the company and major developments in the field; further, since the backgrounds of team members are similar, the communication of these developments is facilitated between members of the department, allowing for relatively efficient knowledge transfer. Hence, the advantage of this type of structure is that transfer of specialized technical information can be performed, allowing the maintenance of high levels of expertise in a given area around which a department has been formed. However, one of the greatest challenges of this type of structure is that often company projects require multiple areas of expertise, and thus, by definition, requires a multifunctional team. Indeed, the technical departmental team tends to have expertise in technology, but does not have similar skills product/program development, which is more market (or "outward") facing.

Key points:

- Departmental technical teams are composed of members in a specialized area with similar backgrounds.
- The proximity to developments in the technical field as well as communication and efficient knowledge transfer within the team is a strength.
- Departmental technical teams are less able to respond to the market because they tend to be focused on technology rather than a specific product or program.

Multidisciplinary Project Team: Addressing the Market

In contrast to departmental teams, whose strength lies in the proximity to the communication of developments in the field, the multidisciplinary team is more "outward" facing, with emphasis on a product/program derived from inputs of a number of disciplines, and developed with perspectives that are not only technical, but also commercially focused. Because the market understands outputs from the company on the basis of what it may consume (rather than the technical expertise resident in the company), this type of approach resonates within environments with which the company operates. In contrast to the departmental teams, however, the level of coordination needed for these multifunctional teams is quite high, since by design the areas of expertise are different and diverse, and yet still require integration and communication in a common language that all members can understand. In the extreme, the members of the team are made resident to the team, and report to the team leader (the supervisor) – this facilitates communication, knowledge transfer, and thus coordination and provides strong bonding to the product/program, and thus to the market. However, the challenge is that the trade-off for this type of structure is the reduction of the interaction of team members within their areas of expertise, which can reduce the level of competence of each team member in their specialty area, since there is less contact with other department of origin members. Indeed, with such a structure, as more members of each department are assigned to project teams and leave the department, the resident expertise of the company diminishes. Moreover, the performance of teams *declines* with time, concurrent with a loss of technical expertise. Hence, project teams have the advantage of reflecting a number of areas of specialization allowing for coordinated product and program development, but at a cost of technical decline.

Key points:

- Transfer of knowledge requires significant coordination in groups with different backgrounds and areas of expertise.
- Multidisciplinary teams coordinate the efforts of different members thus emphasizing product and programs (and thus, the market).
- The trade-off of multidisciplinary teams is the loss of specialized expertise due to proximity to the product/program team rather than the specialized department (of origin).

Matrix Teams: Addressing the Market and Technology

The response to departmental and project team challenges has been the *matrix team* approach, which utilizes concepts from both departmental and project teams, thus (hypothetically) allowing the members to keep their respective expertise, as well as to participate on project teams that are highly coordinated. Each member of a department and team therefore effectively has (at least) two supervisors – one from their home department where their expertise lies, and one from each project/program team he or she is associated with – to which he or she reports. Ideally, this creates a situation where team members can coordinate efforts for product development, yet maintain technical expertise simultaneously. However, at the supervisory level, the matrix team creates tension between the departmental leaders and the project managers, since each has supervisory responsibilities, but different inherent goals – technical expertise *vs.* product development progress, respectively. A technical executive needs to recognize this tension and ensure that the balance between the project teams and the departments is maintained, in order to provide products responsive to the marketplace with the technical integrity ensured by the most recent technological developments. In addition, understanding the demands placed on team members who now have two, or multiple, sets of responsibilities (and supervisors) needs to be clear, in order to avoid loss of both team and technical participation and productivity.

Key points:
- Matrix teams allow for participation of members in both departments and project and program teams.
- Matrix teams effectively create (at least) two supervisors for team members – the department head and the project manager(s).
- Tension between the departments and the project teams requires the technical executive to balance the requirements and goals of both.

"No Messenger Rule"

Boeing's T. Wilson was a pioneer in the matrix management team structure, which continues at the company today. A key component of these teams is the empowerment of the team and its members; as noted, the constant tension between team leaders and functional area heads can lead to paralysis if not managed appropriately. At Boeing, there is a "no messenger rule" where team members are expected to make decisions "on the spot," without going back to functional areas to seek permission. The purpose of this rule is to allow the teams not only to be empowered to make decisions, but to take initiative in day-to-day interactions. Such empowerment and self-management enabled the 777 passenger jet to fly its initial test flight with fewer than half the number of design problems of previous projects, saving millions of dollars in the process.

Dumaine, Brian. The Trouble with Teams. Fortune 130/5, September 5, 1994.

ADDITIONAL READING

Allen, T.J., Henn, G.W., 2007. The Organization and Architecture of Innovation. Butterworth-Heinemann and Architectural Press, Boston.
Cohen, S.G., Baily, D.E., 1997. What makes teams work: group effectiveness research from the shop floor to the executive suite. J. Manag. 3, 239–290.
Sy, T., D'Annunzio, L., 2005. Challenges and strategies of matrix organizations: top-level and mid-level managers' perspectives. Human Resource Planning Journal 28, 39–48.

TEAM CONSTRUCTION

The construction of project teams is a reflection of the project *per se*, but fundamentally emphasizes active collaboration between members of the

Table 4.1 Roles for Team Function

Role	Description
Idea Generating	General analysis and/or synthesis of information to generate ideas
Entrepreneuring/ Championing	Articulating an idea that may be another's for formal approval within an organization
Project Leading	Acting to coordinate and plan activities related to the project or program
Gatekeeping	Assimilating and communicating important information relevant to the team from internal and external environments
Sponsoring/Coaching	Supportive role in the background, acting as a protector, advocate, and mentor

team as a primary objective. As opposed to formalized departmental structures, where a hierarchical (*viz.* vertical) organization exists, productive teams have been found to be best coordinated when strong peer associative (lateral) relationships occur between members. Indeed, building and nurturing this lateral structure is the prime responsibility of the project or program leader, who acts to ensure each component of the project or program is addressed, and the appropriate personnel become members of the team. It is axiomatic that communication, team building, translation (of terminology between differing disciplines), and clarification are all part of the collaborative effort of every team member, and led and encouraged by the project team leader.

However, there are other roles identified that are both logistically important within the team and contribute to the innovation process (Table 4.1); these are roles that are in addition to those associated with the particular areas of expertise each member brings to the team. In fact, these are team roles that are not (typically) necessarily played by a single individual, although a single individual may play multiple roles, and with the progress of the project or program, roles may shift to other individuals. These include *idea generating, entrepreneuring/championing, project leading, gatekeeping,* and *sponsoring/coaching.* Because these roles are not (with the exception of project leading) formal, the technical executive needs to be well aware of these areas to ensure that the team membership includes individuals with the appropriate characteristics and skills, so that not only is the area of expertise covered, but also these critical roles. Otherwise, the team's effectiveness will suffer, and correspondingly, the program or project.

Table 4.2 Components Influencing Team Construction

Component	Level	Ideal Type of Team
Degree of coordination needed	High	Project/Matrix
	Low	Departmental
Rate of change of technology	High	Departmental
	Low	Project/Matrix
Team duration anticipated	Longer	Departmental
	Shorter	Project/Matrix
Rate of change in the marketplace	High	Project/Matrix
	Low	Departmental

Key points:
- The strength of teams is related to lateral, peer to peer relationships.
- The development and maintenance of lateral relationships is the primary responsibility of the project or program leader.
- Informal roles within the team that are relevant to the innovation process within the team include idea generating, entrepreneuring/championing, project leading, gatekeeping, and sponsoring/coaching.

Characteristics Relevant in Team Construction

As noted previously, there are different considerations to be made when determining team construction and individual assignments of personnel for particular program and project teams. In addition to the nature of the project/program, technical areas of expertise, and informal roles, other logistical and environmental factors have a significant influence on the type of team and degree of success such team will engender within a given project (Table 4.2); these include degree of coordination needed within the project ("interdependence"), rate of change of the technology in the field, anticipated duration of the team's existence, and rate of change in the marketplace (see Allen and Henn, 2007 for an excellent review).

Each of these factors influences whether individuals should become members of the project/matrix team, or whether they should remain in departments. If high levels of coordination are required (with relatively stable technology), the project/matrix team is the best option to ensure integration of efforts and interdependencies are addressed; in contrast, low levels of needed coordination imply a limited level of interdependencies, which can be managed within departments. As noted previously, with longer duration teams, there can be significant diminution of both team productivity and technical expertise when all departmental members reside on such teams; in this case, the departmental teams are favored, particularly when changes in the marketplace are slow or minimal. With a high level of change in the marketplace and stable technology, project/matrix teams are favored, due to the need to respond in an "outward" fashion; when technology is changing quickly with a relatively stable marketplace, the departmental structure is favored, to capture the latest technologic innovations in the field. In the case where there is active change in the marketplace and in the technology in the field, where high levels of coordination are required, data suggests that a combination approach is best effected, where team members start on a project/matrix team to develop a working relationship, followed by transition back to the departments to avoid obsolescence. Using this structure, coordination between departments will be facilitated due to the establishment of working relationships. For teams whose duration is prolonged, this process may need to be repeated.

Key points:
- Other factors found to be important in team construction include degree of coordination required, rate of change of technology, team duration, and rate of change of the marketplace.
- In the case of a project where technology and the marketplace are changing quickly and require significant coordination, using project/matrix teams initially followed by departmental teams works to avoid technology obsolescence while facilitating working relationships between departments.

ADDITIONAL READING

Roberts, E.B., Fusfeld, A.R., 1982. Critical functions: needed roles in the innovation process. In: Katz, R. (Ed.), Career Issues in Human Resource Management. Prentice-Hall, Inc., Englewood Cliffs, NJ.
Sapienza, A.M., 2004. Managing Scientists: Leadership Strategies in Scientific Research, second ed. Wiley-Liss, Inc., Hoboken, NJ.

LEADERSHIP DYNAMICS

As noted previously, the management of technical personnel is unlike that in other industries; most individuals who gravitate toward these areas have high degrees of training and often higher educational achievement. While individuals and technical areas vary, a technical executive needs to be cognizant of the implications of his or her role in leading innovation, and motivating professionals within the organization; it is a primary consideration that challenges the best of leaders. Being mindful of these aspects of leadership and management, the technical executive can provide an opportunity to design and implement his or her respective group to maximize productivity and successful product and/or program development.

Management Failure: The Technical Expert

In many organizations, particularly those with a heavy R&D focus, technical experts who participate on teams or provide specific area advice scientifically are often promoted as recognition of their quality performance. Indeed, with this "reward," such individuals may encounter, for the first time, the need to actively manage others. This experience can be quite different from aspects related to laboratory or other scientific activity – there is a transition from a "doing it all approach," dependent only on oneself, to having to rely upon and delegate to others. Badawy studied this transition and found consistent reasons why certain managers fail. The main etiologies of managerial failure in engineers and scientists included poor interpersonal skills as well as the lack of desire to manage. Because these individuals have typically been rewarded and reinforced for their technical competence, they may find it difficult to trust others, particularly new subordinates that they are expected to mentor and to whom they must delegate. This results in a self-reinforcing paradigm that limits both the new manager and reports. They only trust their own judgment, and delegate little; moreover, he or she is not accustomed to managing others, and thus spends more time doing projects than mentoring. This results in little work being delegated, and inadequate opportunity to supervise and evaluate reports, maintaining the lack of trust in subordinates. In addition, other areas identified as creating issues for the transition from technical expert to manager include the dichotomy between objective measurement of science or engineering versus the "soft" intangibles of management; "paralysis by analysis," – i.e., needing all information to be apparent before making decisions (rather than being able to take risks and make decisions with incomplete data); the need to maintain the moniker of expert in a given field, rather than managing to the objective of completing tasks (rather than doing them); and lack of communication due to a more introverted personality. Technical executives need to be cognizant of these potential pitfalls when moving technical area experts into management positions to avoid ineffective performance (by either/both the manager and reports) during the transition.

Badawy MK. Developing Managerial Skills in Engineers and Scientists: Succeeding as a Technical Manager (1982). Van Nostrand Reinhold Co., Inc.: New York.

Table 4.3 Stages of Innovation

Stage	Activities
Recognition	Recognition of technological feasibility and demand
Idea Formulation	Technology and demand fused into a design concept for evaluation
Problem Solving	Experimentation, evaluation, and determination if information readily available
Solution	Solution through invention and/or adoption
Development	Beta testing and scale up
Utilization and Diffusion	Implementation and use

Leading Innovation

Leading innovation has been described as a process including the generation of new or novel ideas, identification of the ones of most promise, and executing development. This process can be articulated through the classic model of Meyers and Marquis (1969), wherein the recognition of technical feasibility and that of demand, as fused, becomes an idea to be evaluated further. The six steps of the innovation model are shown in Table 4.3.

Conceptually, there is an explicit assumption that invention *per se* is *not* innovation, and that innovation must be conceived through the lens (at least initially) of the combination of an understanding of a market need ("demand") and a given technology; a fusion of these together allows for idea formation that can then be tested as a problem. When a solution is found, development ensues, and a successful innovation results from both utilization as well as diffusion in the market. Hence, using this paradigm, the selection and further development of the perceived "best" technology can be performed, and "success" of an innovation is defined as diffusion into the marketplace.

In this context, the technical executive should understand that the process and its results are dynamic, and may require iterations over time (like any R&D project); once programs reach the marketplace, there is an inherent life cycle for such programs, and the management of these projects – and the innovation process – is important to maintain commercial value, with (as required) additional innovations within the product line (as appropriate for the strategy of the firm) (see also Chapters 1 and 7 on Marketing and Product Development, respectively).

In addition, executives need to be quite cognizant that, as products in the marketplace mature, there is a high likelihood (especially in very successful markets) that imitators and "disruptive" innovation may occur (see also Chapter 7). This disruption often if not always occurs *outside* the company in a market segment (currently) unattractive to the firm due to being of relatively low value; these customers may have been forced out of the market for various reasons (e.g. expense), or because their needs have been unarticulated. However, such entrants may pose a future threat to an organization if the technology takes root, even within a small and/or unattractive contingent of the market. While companies with *established* products are typically excellent at *sustaining* innovations, where better products are brought to established markets almost exclusively by industry leaders, disruptive technologies are often brought forth by smaller competitors willing to access the low margin segments with products addressing (at least initially) a niche. Indeed, disruptive technologies need to be recognized, since they have the potential to move upward from the aforementioned initial low margin and unattractive market, *unimpeded by competition by larger providers*, to higher margin, more attractive markets, potentially forcing industry leaders to higher level markets, and eventually when overall revenues have declined to the industry leader, to market exit. Hence, technical executives have the challenge of not only managing the innovation process, but also recognizing potentially disruptive innovations of their businesses. Because of their technical competence, technical executives are uniquely qualified to do this if they recognize the challenge.

Hence, the ability to manage both sustaining innovation as well as radical substitutes of currently available products is a key responsibility of the technical executive. Organizations that can innovate on mature products and businesses but also generate new and novel technologies which can be evaluated and developed (as noted in Table 4.3) (or discarded early, if not found to be experimentally viable), are "ambidextrous" – in other words, they can execute in multiple facets of innovation (sustained and disruptive). As may be inferred, it has been seen that the types of management for these types of competencies is (quite) different; the former is more structured and formal, while the latter requires more of a "skunkworks" or "startup" entrepreneurial mentality. While challenging both on a leadership and managerial scale, the *integration* of the latter into the former is of paramount importance for the firm to both maintain a successful commercial business, and survive the product and process life cycles and innovations.

Key points:

• The stages of innovation can be described to include recognition, idea formation, problem solving, solution, development, utilization, and diffusion.

- Invention and innovation are different; invention or technology with an identified market need starts the process of innovation.
- Technical executives need to be cognizant of both disruptive and sustaining innovations and the difference in management approaches required (the ambidextrous organization).

ADDITIONAL READING

Hoopes, D., 2001. Why are there glitches in product development?. R&D Management 31, 381–389.
Katz, R., Paap, J., 2004. Anticipating disruptive technologies. Research Technology Management 47, 13–22.
Senge, P.M., 1994. The Fifth Discipline: The Art and Practice of the Learning Organization. Doubleday, New York.
Utterback, J., 1994. Mastering the Dynamics of Innovation. Harvard Business School Press, Cambridge.

Motivation

One of the most relevant and most difficult aspects of technical leadership revolves around motivation; it is a key managerial responsibility, and in particular, has distinct characteristics within a technical organization. There are a variety of texts providing an excellent review of the cognitive theories of motivation (see, for example, Katz, *The Motivation of Professionals, in* **The Human Side of Managing Technological Innovation**, 2004).

For the technical executive, the motivation of groups starts with the individual. There are a variety of studies noting the importance of *active listening* for managers, to fully comprehend needs and backgrounds. Creating an environment that takes into account such needs is a fundamental responsibility of technical leadership. Indeed, it is within the context of the technical work environment that these needs are articulated. It has been shown that the *context* of the settings in which individuals work – including the structures, corporate and operational strategies, reward systems, and leadership – significantly influences behavior and focus, which then shape attitudes, manifest by expectations, choices, interpretations, and behavior. As leaders, it is important to recognize that by *designing this context* in which individuals and groups work, the motivation (and thus behavior) of individual employees is influenced, to either drive or kill motivation (and it is significantly easier to do the latter).

Part of the design of a work environment that enhances motivation in technical organizations revolves around the type of work assigned to each individual or group. It has been shown that technical staff, while appreciating financial rewards and prompt career advancement, are far more interested in working on interesting technical projects and/or challenges, and utilizing and developing their abilities within their field of expertise. Further, the nature of the work must have some level of perceived importance in the organization, with diversity of activities to provide an opportunity for additional learning. Inclusion into a project team where there is documented participation, and where success results not only in pride of accomplishment but also peer respect (particularly outside the company) is a key factor in motivating technical professionals. Moreover, it is relevant to be aware of *matches* between articulated and demonstrated staff competencies and job requirements ("fit") within a project team, in order to keep motivation high. In fact, in some cases, where exposure to financial and business concepts and tasks are apparent, this process will allow the technical executive to (self) identify those who have potential to be scientific managers, rather than scientists who emulate managers, to the benefit of the entire organization. And finally, operational autonomy is relevant for individuals and teams to become highly motivated; providing an environment where freedom to make choices *within the execution of goals* enhances both personal responsibility and initiative.

Reward systems, as noted, are also somewhat different with technical staff. Fundamentally, the technical manager should recognize that he or she needs to have credibility in the organization when providing rewards; there needs to be full assurance there is a distinct relationship between *effort* and *outcome*; otherwise, it will be assumed that either capriciousness or cronyism is the source of the reward. Further, in addition to equity and fairness, rewards tend to work best when they are both informal and formal, and delivered on a timely basis; studies have revealed that providing different informal rewards for different types of achievements tends to avoid complacency and the perception of entitlements when recognizing individual or group efforts. Technical staff, because of their background and training, still tend toward their roots within an academic organization − they want to be seen as having an impact, and perceived as being an expert and having solved a difficult problem. Reward systems within technical organizations must take these traits into account.

Key points:
- Active listening and responding with an appropriate work organization provides a motivating environment for technical staff.
- Working on interesting projects/challenges, utilizing and developing abilities, a perceived important project, autonomy, and peer respect are important in motivating technical employees.

- Formal and informal reward systems are appropriate with technical employees and provide motivation in the context of the work environment.

Motivation: Career Anchors

An approach for motivating employees can involve assessing the priorities of staff and how they view their overall work. Edgar Schein articulated the "career anchor," which helps describe ways in which individuals conceptualize work, and how they see themselves fitting into their respective jobs. These include:

- Technical/Functional Competence: See themselves as an expert in an area
- General Managerial Competence: Desires experience in many roles to attain general manager title/responsibility
- Autonomy/Independence: Independent, individual player; perceives freedom from interaction with others with solo effort as a goal
- Security/Stability: Desires defined goals and expectations within the firm
- Entrepreneurial Creativity: Interest is in creating and running an entity
- Sense of Service: Desire to work on a specific service or cause
- Pure Challenge: Fulfillment comes from working on progressively more difficult projects
- Lifestyle: Organize work around private life

Using these anchors as guides, managers can understand the potential aspects which drive employee behavior, as well as provide opportunities for growth and development based on the levels of importance of these components. Two-way communication is of obvious importance to ensure that both the employee articulates his or her priorities to the supervisor, and the supervisor formulates a plan which addresses the employee's career anchor needs in order to improve motivation and productivity.

Schien, Edgar (2007). Career Anchors Revisited: Implications for Career Development in the 21st Century. NHRD Journal 1:27–33.

ADDITIONAL READING

Clark, R.E., 2003. Fostering the work motivation of individuals and teams. Perform. Improv. 42, 21–29.

Katz, R. (Ed.), 2004. The Human Side of Managing Technological Innovation: A Collection of Readings, second ed., Oxford University Press, New York.

Manso, G., 2011. Motivating innovation. Journal of Finance 66, 1823–1860.

CHANGE MANAGEMENT

Change is a natural aspect of the managerial function as well as part of the development and responsiveness of any organization. However, as natural as change is to any firm, the resistance to change is also as pervasive, and something which the technical executive needs not only to be mindful of, but prepared for when change is afoot. Indeed, a huge component of change management is the firm and unyielding grip of the *status quo*, particularly in perceived entrepreneurial organizations where culture is especially strong ("we've never done it that way before"). While given processes or procedures may be admitted to being poorly conceived or even inefficient, they may be so engrained that altering behavior may be perceived as too high of a barrier to consider. Further, particularly in technical organizations where delegation and ramifications of proposed change is not entirely clear, there may be significant reticence toward action related to change due to perceived risk (see the sidebar "Managerial Failure: The Technical Expert" earlier in this chapter). This can even turn the tables, reinforcing the notion that change is unnecessary. As part of this dedication toward the *status quo*, resistance to change may also be related to the lack of communication of change agents providing a vehicle of commonality of purpose ("coordinating device"). Affected members of the organization, particularly in technical organizations where "hard" data is emphasized, must be able to see how changes impact them concretely, if not at the defined day-to-day level, then at the strategic or directional level. If this is not provided, studies have shown change initiatives will often fail (Nimmo and Holland, 2000). This can then lead to a torrid self-fulfilling prophecy in which change initiatives "all fail," cynicism settles in, and the *status quo* is further strengthened. As a result, change and change management becomes at best a Sisyphean task.

To manage change as a technical executive, as noted, a fundamental and clear articulation of rationale is important for facilitating a dialogue with those affected. Having a tangible understanding on how and why change will affect persons within the organization will allow further practical approaches and engagement by both management and staff on change implementation. Maintaining motivation is key in this endeavor; low morale is associated with low flexibility and openness to new ideas. In contrast, creating a sense of urgency, ensuring consistency of policies and infrastructure to support the change, and putting in place tangible milestones and feedback mechanisms (including plan-do-study-act cycles; see

Chapter 8 on Operations) can have significantly beneficial reinforcements for change. This includes sponsorship from senior executives who have identified change as important for the entire organization or a part of it, with a high level of visibility before, during, and after the process. Hence, while change can be difficult, the technical executive should be aware that communication, preparation, involvement, feedback, and sponsorship are necessary to successfully implement change.

Key points:

• Resistance to change is often mired in the tenacious grip of the *status quo*, perceived risk, and reinforced cynicism.
• Technical staff may be particularly reticent to accept change given that they are accustomed to "hard" and complete data before making decisions.
• An unmotivated staff will be less likely to be open to change.
• Utilizing approaches where preparation, communication, sponsorship, and tangible impact are clear provides an environment with the most potential for sustained change.

ADDITIONAL READING

Kotter, J.P., 1996. Leading Change. Harvard Business School Press, Cambridge.
Lorenzi, N.M., Riley, R.T., 2000. Managing change: an overview. Journal American Medical Inform Assoc 7, 116–124.
Nimmo, C., Holland, R.W., 2000. Transitions in Pharmacy Practice, Part 5: Walking the tightrope of change. Am J Health Syst Pharm 57, 64–72.

GENERAL REFERENCES AND WEBSITES ON LEADERSHIP AND MANAGEMENT

Flamholtz, E.G., Randle, Y., 2007. Growing Pains: Transitioning From an Entrepreneurship to a Professionally Managed Firm. Jossey-Bass, San Francisco.
Meyers, S., Marquis, D.G., 1969. Successful Industrial Innovations. National Science Foundation, Washington D. C.
Smircich, L., Morgan, G., 1982. Leadership: the management of meaning. Journal Applied Behavioral Science 18, 257–273.
Chief Executive, <http://chiefexecutive.net/>. (accessed 16 August 2012)
Harvard Business Review Magazine, <http://hbr.org/>. (accessed 12 June 2012)
MIT Sloan Management Review Magazine, <http://sloanreview.mit.edu/>. (accessed 12 June 2012)
Strategy + Business Magazine, <http://www.strategy-business.com/>. (accessed 2 July 2012)

CHAPTER 5

Portfolio Management

Table of Contents

"I would say that what we've gotten for a half a billion dollars is an unpronounceable acronym [DIMHRS]."

Robert Gates

"My personal philosophy is not to undertake a project unless it is manifestly important and nearly impossible."

Edwin Land

INTRODUCTION

"Portfolio management" (understood as the management of assets to provide the largest return), whether articulated as such or under other monikers, has been an activity performed in one way or another by technical executives in the management of projects for many years. On a corporate level, while many of the concepts are similar to those derived from

The Pragmatic MBA for Scientific and Technical Executives
DOI: http://dx.doi.org/10.1016/B978-0-12-397932-2.00005-3

R&D project decisions, the actual activities performed may vary given the other parts of the organization and factors requiring consideration within the portfolio. Much of portfolio management theory comes from that described for the construction of financial portfolios, i.e., maximizing a return of a chosen set of assets given a level of risk, or alternatively, minimizing risk for a specified level of return (e.g., "modern portfolio theory"). These activities are typically performed by combining assets with different weightings, and using diversification to minimize risk below any individual asset chosen within the portfolio. In portfolio management of projects, the concept is similar: choose programs and projects whose combination maximizes return and minimizes risk for the organization. However, while relatively simple in concept, there are many potential challenges to ensure that not only are the appropriate projects placed into a portfolio, but that the level of integration and support allow for optimization as well.

It is clear this aspect of corporate planning is becoming more relevant, manifest by the vast numbers of evaluation platforms and programs which have found their way into firms. Nonetheless, and importantly, the paradigms are very similar, and relate to evaluation of the risk and return of a set of choices of the firm as they match against strategic imperatives. While the mathematical formulations of modern portfolio theory in finance cannot be stringently matched with programs and projects within a company, the basic concepts of identifying risk, understanding diversification, and weighting (project and program) components based on strategic objectives (of the company) allow the construction of a portfolio that can maximize value for the company.

COMMON TRAITS

As noted earlier, there are a myriad of different platforms that have been created to facilitate portfolio management, with the requisite implementation and rollout teams willing to train companies in their use. Again, the fundamental goal of this process is to ensure that the company chooses a portfolio that will maximize value and minimize risk to the firm. As such, there are some key common components relevant toward this fundamental goal and of which the technical executive should be aware:

1. *Standardized measures.* Portfolio management processes must be able to translate the corporate strategy into measurable outputs, to allow comparisons amongst programs and projects. Without this as a pillar of

the process, the assessment of choices becomes at best difficult, and at worst self-deceiving.

2. *Resource allocation.* By definition, the resources existing in a company are limited. An understanding of the resources available for allocation is needed to determine the components that will be appropriate for the portfolio.

3. *Defining and evaluating risk.* Project costs and cash flows, as well as the effect of optionality (managerial flexibility) need to be outlined for the portfolio management process. Timing and degree of resource allocation are both relevant in this aspect of the process. Both projects that are ongoing, as well as those that have been chosen *not* to move forward are important in this assessment.

4. *Portfolio tracking.* As portfolio management is the continuous process of identifying and managing a number of projects that should add value to the firm, having methods that can clearly determine the progress of each project, and therefore the portfolio, is relevant.

5. *Communication.* The ability to communicate the results of the portfolio management process, its outcomes, and ongoing evaluation(s) is important to maintain learning advantages to the organization as the portfolio and projects move through their respective life cycles.

These components should be familiar to the R&D executive, as they represent the basics that a portfolio management process needs to encompass in order to be effective. Inherent in this set of parameters is the *interaction* of the components of any portfolio, in order to have a true synergy of these parts. Indeed, it is these measurable synergies that provide the portfolio competitive advantage (or a core competency or extended enterprise; see Chapter 3 on Corporate Strategy), when matched against the company strategy

Key points:

- Common parameters to be considered in the portfolio management process include standardization, resource allocation, assessing risk, portfolio tracking, and clear communication.
- The true synergies of a portfolio are based on the interaction of the component parts to drive value.

ADDITIONAL READING

Cooper, R.G., Edgett, S.J., Kleinschmidt, E.J., 2001. Portfolio Management for New Products. Perseus Publishing, Cambridge.

Bahadur, N., Landry, E., Treppo, S., 2006. How to slim down a brand portfolio. Strategy + Business 44, 4–6.

CONSIDERATIONS IN PORTFOLIO MANAGEMENT
Strategic Alignment and Execution

All models of portfolio management need to align with the strategy of the organization. Every project or program axiomatically should be tied back to the corporate strategy when making decisions. The challenge with strategic alignment and portfolio management revolves around the existence of competing portfolios matching the firm's needs, yet a limited amount of resources that cannot encompass all choices. As such, modern corporate portfolio management emphasizes *continuing evaluation* of the programs and projects, encompassing choices made by senior leaders including technical executives. Because the business environment is both complex and ever-changing, a static portfolio management process does not leverage the continuing *learnings of the organization* within a program or project, if not constantly reevaluated. Indeed, most portfolio management approaches include diagnostic approaches, which articulate milestone and decision points where operational considerations can be evaluated. Hence, the ability to learn from programs and projects within an organization in a dynamic fashion, with a constant reference to the strategic goals of an organization, is a paramount goal by which the portfolio management process encompasses and drives within successful companies. Not surprisingly, the linkage between the *strategic process* and the *portfolio management process* has been noted as a factor in the successful implementation of corporate strategy in a variety of different types of firms. By ensuring programs and projects are in alignment with the corporate strategy, the execution of the strategic imperatives of the company become more clear.

Key points:

- The first step in portfolio management is to have a clear understanding of the corporate strategy.
- The portfolio management process is dynamic and encompasses the learnings of the organization.
- Linking the strategic process with the portfolio management process provides the firm the best opportunity to execute on its corporate strategy successfully.

Talking Different Languages: Strategic Issues and the Airbus A380

The Airbus A380 development project was begun prior to its main competitor, the Boeing 787 Dreamliner. Nonetheless, the 787 project was completed and launched in July 2007, when the A380 was already two years behind schedule. The failure of Airbus, despite having the development lead, was part and parcel of poor corporate strategy, communication, team management, and project control. Issues had arisen as early as 2006; German, French, British, and Spanish parts of the organization were struggling for control; a negotiated internal "settlement" occurred where Airbus was consolidated under "co-CEOs," one located in France, and the other in Germany. Despite this, struggles continued to occur, and this trickled down into project teams, where French and German teams worked independently, with the company being required to work out independent labor agreements in both countries. Indeed, French workers accused the German team members of covering up or ignoring problems to keep work inside Germany. Design computers used by engineers did not show the same information or speak the same language, delaying redesigns of existing parts or new designs. Even with directives from top management in Germany to use a single design system, project team engineers continued to use earlier generation systems that tended to distort results. The failure in program and portfolio management as well as team oversight resulted in inconsistent tools and computer software and hardware, and constant bickering. This created delays and significant hurdles to completing the A380 project at breakeven rates, based on forecasted numbers of planes to be purchased. The delays resulted in highly critical external audits by customers, and cancelled or significantly delayed orders by FedEx, Virgin Airways, Lufthansa, and Emirates.

The share price dropped by 26% when the second delay was announced, and both of the CEOs departed. It was estimated that Airbus destroyed at least $6.1B in operating profit value through these delays. As of November 2011, there were 238 firm orders for the A380, 60 of which had been delivered; it was estimated that Airbus would need to sell 420 units (2006 dollars) to break even on the development of the plane.

Garfein S. Executive Guide to Strategic Portfolio Management: Roadmap for Closing the Gap between Strategy and Results. PMI Global Congress Proceedings, Atlanta, GA, 2007. www.airbus.com/company/ market/orders deliveries/, November 14, 2011.

ADDITIONAL READING

Cameron, B.H., 2006. IT portfolio management: implementing and maintaining IT strategic alignment. In: Walters, B., Tang, Z (Eds.), IT Enabled Strategic Management: Increasing Returns for the Organization. IGI Global, Hershey.

Iamratanakul, S., Shankar, R., Dimmitt, N.J., 2009. Improving project portfolio management with strategic alignment. Management of Engineering and Technology 2, 1290–1300.

Resource Allocation

Fundamentally, portfolio management is an exercise in assessing corporate needs vis-à-vis strategy, resulting in allocation of resources to different component parts within an organization. Each component of the organization is considered an asset, which adds value to the organization in one way or another (tacitly on a strategic or revenue basis). As such, the portfolio of assets is *not* solely about the generation of cash, but potentially also about development of (core) capabilities, pipeline, resources, or an extended enterprise – it is a more broad set of components that create the most value for the firm to meet strategic objectives. In this way, corporate portfolio management differs from individual project portfolio management (often called "pipeline management"), in that assets are defined differently and considered in a manner that allows comparisons to be made in accordance with corporate strategy. After corporate strategy, this component of portfolio management represents the ensuing step in order to start the process of creating a portfolio of projects contemplating the objectives of the firm.

Key points:

- Resource allocation is a key component and one manifestation of the portfolio management process.
- Projects and programs within the portfolio management process are not only those that generate cash, but also any aspect within the firm that addresses the strategic goals and objectives of the firm.

ADDITIONAL READING

Cooper, R.G., Edgett, S.J., Kleinschmidt, E.J., 2004, Sept–Oct. Benchmarking best NPD practices–II. Research-Technology Management, 50–59.

Kavadias, S., Chao, R.O., 2007. Resource allocation and new product development portfolio management. In: Loch, C.H., Kavadias, S. (Eds.), Handbook of New Product Development Research. Elsevier/Butterworth, Oxford.

Impact

The level of impact of a given portfolio is based on the choices made within each individual project, where the aim is to ensure the sum of the parts is greater than the respective components. Conceptually, the impact of the portfolio should be an improvement in operational performance, which in turn impacts the achievement of the company's internal and external deliverables. As noted, these are important to monitor, in that course corrections can be made as appropriate given tangible measures that have been identified during the portfolio management process. For commercial projects, common measures such as net present value (NPV), free cash flow, forecasted cash flow, etc. are all used (but see the "Real Options" later in the chapter); for other internal projects, meeting developmental goals, milestones, capabilities, and other aspects of projects are relevant. A key aspect to this component is clearly articulating the *target being measured* (with given resource and time parameters). As noted previously, without standardization by which projects and programs can be measured, it is difficult at best to determine progress, and decide whether the portfolio is performing at the desired level (and whether decisions need be made regarding changes, if any). Finally, while there are many ways to evaluate the progress of the components of the portfolio, ensuring that there is an understanding of the potential synergistic *interaction* of each program and project, as well as the opportunity costs of resourced programs and projects (*vs.* nonresourced ones) should be highly visible within the organization to assess the impact of the total portfolio toward company objectives.

Key points:

- The impact of the portfolio is manifest by operational performance and the achievement of internal and external measurable deliverables.
- Measures of impact are related to the type of project and program being considered.
- Relationships between projects derived from the portfolio management process, as well as any opportunity costs associated with the choices made within the portfolio, should be regularly evaluated to ensure the impact toward firm objectives is clear.

ADDITIONAL READING

Jeffery, M., Leliveld, I., 2004. Best practices in IT portfolio management. MIT Sloan Management Review 45, 41–49.

Rodrigues Tavares, L., Santiago, L.P., Vakili, P., 2010. Portfolio management of new products and the impact of manager's heuristic during the development process. Technology Management for Global Economic Growth 18, 1–10.

Weill, P., Aral, S., 2006. Generating premium returns on your IT investments. MIT Sloan Management Review 47, 39–48.

Pipeline Construction

An important output of any portfolio management process is a pipeline of projects, typically a mix of new and ongoing efforts within the organization. For the technical executive, the implicit meaning of such an exercise will be the resultant resources available for product development, and the necessary choices that will need to be made which will best match the corporate goals and strategy. More specifically, the implications include the types of innovations to take forward (given success rates in the industry), such as whether to use new product or line extension strategies, what stages of programs should be supported to ensure proper timing of product introduction into the marketplace (and thus revenues), and the types of efforts within business development to facilitate the creation of the portfolio to match the needed pipeline to execute upon the corporate strategy. Additionally, infrastructure considerations manifest as projects to support these efforts are part of the portfolio management process and pipeline construction, creating a base by which these multiple projects can coexist.

Key point:

- The pipeline of programs and projects is another direct manifestation of the portfolio management process.

ADDITIONAL READING

Levine, H.A., 2005. Project Portfolio Management: A Practical Guide to Selecting Projects, Managing Portfolios and Maximizing Benefits. Jossey-Bass, San Francisco.

MODELS FOR PORTFOLIO MANAGEMENT

Decision Analysis

The use of decision analysis in portfolio management is one of the major applications of this area of work. Decision analysis represents the application of a set of tools that allows for the assessment of the cost and value of projects within and subsequently of an entire portfolio. As such, decision analysis provides a fundamental technique ("toolbox") for formally assessing a portfolio through understanding each decision step, collecting information, assessing risk, identifying and evaluating alternatives, and communicating and executing derived decisions. These components are always estimated by evaluating the full range of alternatives available, accounting for the defined consequences of each decision to be made along the pathway of each alternative, and the desired outcome.

Decision analysis can be manifest using graphical representations, particularly *influence diagrams* and *decision trees* (see Figure 5.1). These diagrams describe the alternatives for any decision maker, using probabilities and descriptions of risk manifest by a description of *utility* (e.g., revenues). The

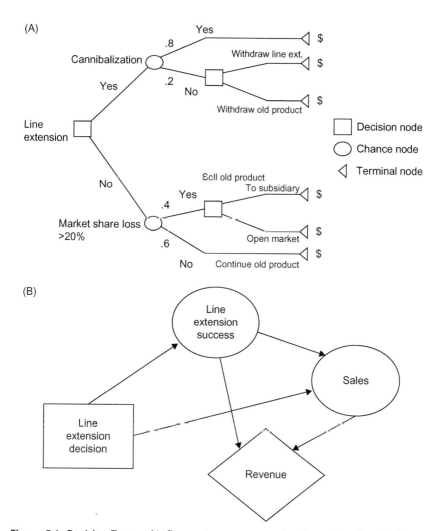

Figure 5.1 Decision Tree and Influence Diagram Examples. A. Decision Tree. *Each pathway represents a scenario; chance nodes (circles) are uncertainties or risks having probabilities; squares represent decisions to be made. Trianges are at times used as terminal nodes (final outcome). Branches emanating from each are by definition nonoverlapping outcomes or decisions, respectively. B. Influence Diagram. In this depiction, squares represent decisions, ovals represent an action, and the diamond represents a result.*

decision tree captures a problem by structuring choices with the end being a payoff of some sort associated with a pathway or scenario; subjective probabilities are assigned to choices (*chance nodes*) from decisions made (*decision nodes*). There are *payoffs* for each scenario, which can be based on the compilation of decisions and choices made; these payoffs can be analyzed in many different ways (e.g., one direction, both directions, through Monte Carlo simulation, etc.), both individually or encompassing the entire scenario/path. Similarly, an influence diagrams shows the problem (i.e., portfolio combinations), but reveals the dependencies of the variables more simply than the extensive decision tree; it is a compact representation of the decision tree, with the representation of the influence of each area on another. By evaluating courses of action (alternatives) and quantifying the probabilities of achieving various alternatives, decisions can be made that define the pathway of decisions that maximize the expected desired utility. As such, the decision analysis constructs a value model that not only outlines the various alternatives, but also how they perform, *via* the defined evaluation metrics. The use of other techniques, which in and of themselves are used for portfolio management, are part of the toolbox of decision analysis (e.g., multiattribute analysis, real options; see below).

Key points:

- Decision analysis is the application of a set of tools that can be used in portfolio management by applying decision analytical techniques to proposed projects or project combinations within a portfolio to define cost and value.
- The identification of alternatives and the quantification of each decision step or outcome are key components of decision analysis.

ADDITIONAL READING

Skinner, D.C., 2009. Introduction to Decision Analysis, third ed. Probabilistic Publishing, Gainsville.
Walls, M.R., 2004. Combining decision analysis and portfolio management to improve project selection in the exploration and production firm. J Petroleum Science Engineering 44, 55–65.

Real Options

A key component of the portfolio management process is the assessment and assignment of risk. There are a variety of ways to do this, all of which are based on a need to understand the basic cost-benefits of any choices made within the portfolio and the portfolio management process. Traditionally, the use of NPV of programs and projects has been the gold standard for quantifying risk, based on calculations of various forms of cost of capital and forecasted cash flows. However, this approach assumes that all future cash flows will be *static*, and it will not encompass the various decisions that can be made by management, as more information becomes known with the progression of the project. Hence, the *NPV analysis will always underestimate project value*, and emphasize the lowest risk programs with the smallest cash outlay. Static discounted cash flow does *not* take into account the managerial flexibility inherent in companies, and penalizes projects with higher risk but also with greater flexibility. By considering an *option model*, where management has the option (although not the obligation) to invest (or not) at a given time, changes in cash flows result, and limit the downside aspect of investment in a project (funds are cut off from the program) while increasing or allowing investments in projects that continue to achieve milestones (and presumably result in positive future cash flow). This managerial flexibility as *an option to invest* in a project and program can be modeled using financial call options (e.g., the Black-Scholes model), and acts as an excellent supplement to standard discounted cash flow approaches, particularly in projects within R&D, to demonstrate the value of such flexibility. This *real option* approach is imperative for technical executives to understand, in order to more accurately show the overall value of key programs and projects, and how they add to a given portfolio being considered for resource allocation.

Key points:

- NPV analysis underestimates project value because of the assumption of static future cash flows.
- Real options relate to managerial flexibility, where there is a call option to invest in a project which may or may not be exercised.
- While discounted cash flow gives some information on relative risk, equal weight is given to optimistic and pessimistic scenarios, where in fact management will discard the pessimistic scenarios and not further invest.
- A real options model is an important aspect to construct any portfolio as it better reflects the options management has for the portfolio and component parts and thus diminishes biases inherent in NPV analysis.

ADDITIONAL READING

Angelou, G.N., Economides, A.A., 2005. Flexible ICT investments analysis using real options. Int Journal of Technology, Policy and Management 5, 146–166.

Sanwal, A., 2007. Optimizing Corporate Portfolio Management: Aligning Investment Proposals with Organizational Strategy. John Wiley & Sons, Hoboken, NJ.

Yeo, K.T., Qiu, F., 2003. The value of management flexibility–a real option approach to investment evaluation. International Journal of Project Management 21, 243–250.

Multiattribute Utility Analysis

Multiattribute utility analysis (MAUA) is used to define the attributes important in a given decision to create value, based on the summation of the subjective assessment of these attributes. MAUA theory is a systematic approach quantifying preferences. In this context, it may be used to rescale a numerical value on some measure of interest onto a given scale, for example, 1 to 5, with 1 being the lowest weighting for an attribute, and 5 representing the most important of attributes. Similarly, the different alternatives being considered would be evaluated with respect to these attributes, e.g., −2 to +2, with −2 representing the least preferred preference and +2 being the most desirable (see Figure 5.2). Using such a scale, a direct comparison of many diverse attributes can be made. This allows a rank-ordered evaluation of alternatives to be constructed reflecting a *decision maker preference*. Indeed, as preferences of the relevance of the attributes differ for different decision makers, the outcome of a MAUA decision (e.g., portfolio composition) may vary, depending on who makes the decisions regarding each attribute. There are a number of different MAUA methodologies available; nonetheless, they are similar in that each attribute that is considered to be important is analyzed separately for *utility* (value, or satisfaction; see also Chapter 1 on Marketing) for each alternative; these are combined with a given weighting based on the relative importance of each attribute, and then combined to provide a sum and ranking. The process therefore involves the separation of attributes initially, with the metrics defined for each, with attendant scores. As noted, weighting needs to be defined for these attributes, since it is assumed that each attribute does not

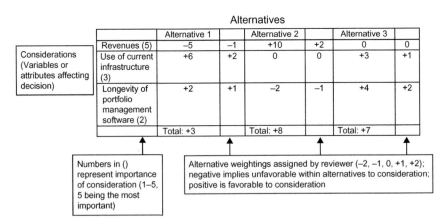

Figure 5.2 *Example of Multiattribute Utility Analysis.* *Nominal overall value (utility) is derived by multiplying importance of consideration (variables or attributes) by weighting of alternatives with respect to that consideration, and summing. In this case, Alternative 2 has the highest utility for this decision maker.*

have equal importance in the overall utility of the decision (i.e., portfolio construction). Using this approach, each alternative generates a single value or utility number representing that particular scenario.

Key points:

- Multiattribute utility analysis allows for quantification of portfolio and project value based on assigning nominal values for single attributes and combining these to produce an overall score.
- The use of subjective measures is key in the utilization of multiattribute utility analysis.
- Direct comparisons between alternatives is a major benefit of this approach in decision analysis and portfolio management.

ADDITIONAL READING

Bichler, M., 2000. An experimenal analysis of multi-attribute auctions. Decision Support Systems 29, 249–268.

Torrance, G.W., Michael, H., Boyle, M.H., Horwood, S.P., 1982. Application of multi-attribute utility theory to measure social preferences for health states. Operations Research 30, 1043–1069.

Modern Portfolio Theory

As noted earlier, modern portfolio theory (MPT) was developed to evaluate markets and investments with the aim of deriving a portfolio containing the largest returns with the lowest risk. The fundamental tenet of MPT is that the evaluation of only one stock's risk and return is not the optimal investment vehicle; rather, by investing in more than one stock, an investor can reduce risk. This moderation of risk is called *diversification*. Risk can be defined as *systematic* or *nonsystematic*; investors are only rewarded by diversifying away an individual company's or group of companies' *nonsystematic* risk (by increasing the number of stocks within a portfolio which do not correlate together in a market). Systematic risk is defined as that inherent within markets, which *cannot* be diversified away; examples include interest rate risk or political instability risk. Nonsystematic risk is that dependent upon the individual investment within which the company or industry exist (e.g., strike of manufacturing employees; unfavorable litigation). Portfolio construction is based on evaluating different stocks, their relative nonsystematic risks, and creating various options, which can be plotted as return *vs.* risk. This results in an *efficient frontier* (Figure 5.3) by which alternatives can be considered

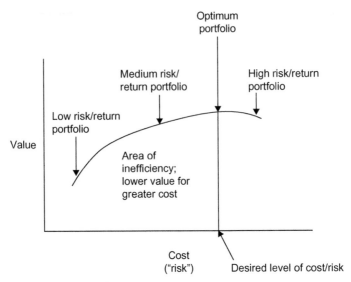

Figure 5.3 *Example of an Efficient Frontier.*

depending on the desired level of risk; for both financial investors, as well as technical (and other) executives constructing internal portfolios, it is the efficient portfolio that provides the most insight.

As noted earlier, the portfolio may consist of various components supporting the corporate strategy of the firm. These assets are used to deliver value, be that in revenues, development of resources, or capabilities for the firm. In this case, the portfolio being created is based on putting together assets (like a financial investor would put together stocks) in differing proportions, and determining the relative risk (often reflected as cost) and return of these alternatives. It is important to know whether the assets will change together, or be *correlated*; it is axiomatic that diversification works to reduce risk by having assets which are not or poorly correlated in a given business context. By assessing these alternatives to construct an efficient frontier of internal assets, a technical executive (and other senior managers) can visualize which portfolio would be appropriate for a given level of risk. While not all asset values may be translatable into similar metrics (e.g., NPV, option value), the use of other measures within decision analysis parameters (e.g., multi-attribute utility analysis) will allow the construction of an efficient frontier.

Key points:
- Modern portfolio theory is based on the premise that risk can be reduced by diversification.
- An efficient frontier can be constructed which shows value per unit risk.
- Creation of an internal efficient frontier by evaluating return *vs.* risk (e.g., cost) can provide guidance on the construction of portfolios for the firm.

ADDITIONAL READING

Brown, J.R., 2010. Managing the retail format portfolio: an application of modern portfolio theory. Journal of Retailing and Consumer Services 17, 19–28.

Krishnan, V., Ulrich, K.T., 2001. Product development decisions: a review of the literature. Manag. Sci. 47, 1–21.

Portfolio Optimization Theory

Portfolio optimization is based on the tenet that most portfolios need to satisfy multiple dimensions ("constraints") when being evaluated, and reflects a more holistic approach to the construction of portfolios than other approaches that utilize a ranking or prioritization approach on a single or limited metric of value. Indeed, portfolio optimization theory does not assign values or ranks *per se* to individual projects, but rather only includes projects or programs if they fit within the constraints identified by the decision maker regarding the needs of the portfolio. This is both the strength and the weakness of this approach; it fits the portfolio into the constraints articulated, but does not value each project on its individual merits; the only aspect to be considered is the constraints that have been drawn into the system. Logistically, this type of analysis can be very helpful when a large number of possibilities exist, either in the numbers of constraints, the number of projects or programs being considered, or both. Examples of constraints might be things such as including projects in a specific demographic, including at least two international projects, having the lowest expenditures on a global scale, and/or maximizing the use of the budget. Usually there is a need to use fairly sophisticated computer modeling, as the constraints and projects being considered generate many (thousands or even millions) potential portfolios. While this type of analysis may require high levels of computing power, it has the ability to generate a number of different portfolios that might not have been considered by decision makers *a priori*, particularly when the numbers of constraints and projects/programs are large. It is usual that a *set* of portfolios is generated, which reflect those encompassing as many of the constraints as possible, but identify key trade-offs between different portfolio solutions. These different portfolio solutions can be *Pareto optimized*, wherein any increase in one constraint trades off and decreases an aspect of another constraint. As a result, key managerial considerations can be made at this juncture once such portfolios are identified.

Key points:

• Portfolio optimization theory considers multiple constraints in order to formulate a portfolio.

• Projects or programs *per se* are not valued individually, but only as a member of a given portfolio.

• The individual components of a portfolio are valuable only in the context that they fit into the constraints articulated.

ADDITIONAL READING

Blau, G.E., Pekny, J.F., Varma, V.A., Bunch, P.R., 2009. Managing a portfolio of interdependent new product candidates in the pharmaceutical industry. Journal of Product Innovation Management 21, 227–245.

Loch, C., Kavadias, S., 2002. Dynamic portfolio selection of NPD programs using marginal returns. Management Science 48, 1227–1241.

GENERAL REFERENCES IN PORTFOLIO MANAGEMENT

Cooper, R.G., Edgett, S.J., Kleinschmidt, E.J., 2000. New problems, new solutions: making portfolio management more effective. Research-Technology Management 43, 18–33.

Cusmano, M.A., Nobeoka, K., 1998. Thinking Beyond Lean: How Project Management Is Transforming Product Development at Toyota and Other Companies. Simon and Shuster, New York.

Dickinson, M.W., Thornton, A.C., Graves, S., 2001. Technology portfolio management: optimizing interdependent projects over multiple time periods. IEEE Transactions on Engineering Management 48, 518–527.

Wynstra, F., ten Pieick, E., 2000. Managing supplier involvement in new product development: a portfolio approach. European Journal of Purchasing and Supply Management 6, 49–57.

CHAPTER 6

Finance and Accounting

Table of Contents

> *"It has been my experience that competency in mathematics, both in numerical manipulations and in understanding its conceptual foundations, enhances a person's ability to handle the more ambiguous and qualitative relationships that dominate our day-to-day financial decision-making."*
>
> ***Alan Greenspan***

> *"The pen is mightier than the sword, but no match for the accountant."*
>
> ***Jonathan Glancey***

INTRODUCTION

Most technical executives are all too familiar with the budgeting process, and that this rolls up into a generalized corporate budget, reflecting the priorities of the company. Nonetheless, the *mechanism* of such a process, where individual budgets become strategic imperatives, may be less certain, and there may be a perception that there is a "black box" by which the finance function of the company turns such efforts into an incomprehensible spreadsheet. Indeed, even the term "finance" often strikes a chord of fear (and loathing) within technical executives, arguably as a result of use of different acronyms, vocabulary, and reporting structures (which are as unfamiliar to the technical executive as compiler theory or the role of NFkb in inflammation is to the finance staff). In fact, finance represents the lab notebook of the firm; it documents both that which has occurred in the company with respect to the accounting measures of resource expenditure, and also puts forth various options and plans for the use of resources in the future.

There are broadly two types of finance with which a technical executive should be familiar: *financial accounting* and *managerial finance*. Financial accounting is the measure of how a firm has performed during some defined time period, and is primarily a *historical* evaluation for *external* parties, such as investors, analysts, and/or governments. Much of the time (particularly in publicly traded companies) the format for such reporting is legally governed by *generally accepted accounting principles* (GAAP), a standardized structure to prevent those evaluating the company's finances from being deceived or misled. Hence, *financial accounting is a backward looking reporting of historical performance primarily aimed at outside audiences.*

In contrast, managerial finance is used for providing information for those responsible for company decision making and planning for future operations; as such, it is directed toward an internal audience of managers. Such reporting is not required by law, and emphasizes flexibility, tailored to evaluate how the firm, projects, or departments are performing and in general the strategic success (or failure) of a firm in the past and scenario planning for the future. Managerial finance, because of its orientation towards the future, very much requires inputs from all parts of the organization (e.g., budgets as noted, sales goals and forecasts, new product launches, etc.) and evaluates alternatives and constraints by which the firm can plot its future strategy. Hence, managerial finance is a forward looking function, which is primarily used for decision making by individuals and groups inside the firm.

Generally speaking, finance communication can be considered through three main documents ("financial statements"): the balance sheet, the income statement, and the cash flow statement. With these instruments, financial performance can be assessed and forecasting can be carried out, using concepts such as ratios and discounted cash flows. Familiarity with these concepts will allow the technical executive to better appreciate how budgets are used within the firm, and will provide an additional tool to assess both corporate and business unit performance within the company.

The Cash Register

While double entry accounting no doubt has been one of the most important inventions in business (originating from Italy from before 1211, and documented almost 300 years later by Pacioli), arguably without the other relevant invention to keep track of financial transactions – the cash register – we might not be using this system of accounting as effectively (or at all). Invented in 1879 by James Ritty, the cash register allowed merchants not only to determine cash flow (and whether employees were stealing from their employers) but also, in concert with double entry bookkeeping, to determine whether they were generating profits or losses. Indeed, without the technological advance of a machine that could record and add, double entry bookkeeping may not have had the same impact as it has had since the innovation was developed.

Ka-ching! Ka-ching! The History of Cash Registers. www.moah.org/kaching.html

FINANCIAL STATEMENTS

The Balance Sheet

Basically, the balance sheet shows the assets and liabilities of the company at a specific time. It is a "snapshot," where someone has (presumably figuratively) travelled the company and put a value on all of the assets of the company, and similarly, evaluated all of what the company owes or will owe. The key concept here is that the assets and liabilities of a given company must always match, or "balance" (hence the name). Some definitions:

Assets: That which a company owns or has claim to; assets can be represented by the formula

$$\text{assets} = \text{liabilities} + \text{shareholder equity}$$

Liabilities: A company's obligations to pay or deliver something of value in the future.

Adding the term "current" to each of the above (arbitrarily) indicates that which can be turned into cash (assets) or must be paid (liabilities) within one year.

Payables: Money owed to parties outside the company.

Receivables: Money owed from parties outside the company.

Shareholder equity: The assets of the company minus the liabilities (*viz.* what the company owns subtracted by what the company owes, by definition); this tends to be a challenging concept for some, but it is just the accounting or "book" estimate of the shareholder value of investment in the company. (Note that shareholder equity may bear little or no relationship to the actual market value of the equity of the company! An example is a successful biotech company with a drug prior to approval – it may have a small shareholder's equity or "book value" due to the accumulated losses of drug development but may have a large market value since this reflects the anticipation of the drug's success.)

Depreciation: A method showing how much of an asset's life is "used up"; in financial accounting terms, allocating the cost of an asset over its useful life.

Table 6.1 shows an example of a balance sheet of a fictional company, TechCo.

Note that any transaction will always have a "double entry" on the balance sheet to keep both sides equal. This is a key rule of financial accounting: any transaction, whether increasing assets (e.g., purchasing a $1000 piece of equipment, where property, plant, and equipment (PP&E) will increase by $1000 and shareholder equity will decrease by $1000) or taking out a $10,000 loan (where cash will increase by $10,000, and debt liabilities will increase by $10,000) is always recorded twice to keep in balance. Again, this shows the company's financial picture at a moment in time (typically at the end of an accounting period such as a quarter or a fiscal year).

Table 6.1 Balance Sheet of TechCo, End of Year 20XX

Assets		Liabilities and Shareholder Equity	
Current assets:		Current liabilities:	
Cash	10,000	Accounts payable	2,000
Accounts receivable	9,000	Income tax payable	4,000
Inventory	500		
Total current assets	19,500	*Total current liabilities*	6,000
		Long-Term debt	500
		Other Long-Term Liabilities	500
Fixed assets			1,000
Land	30,000	Shareholder Equity	
Property, Plant, Equipment	100,000	Common stock	55,000
Accumulated depreciation	(50,000)	Retained earnings	37,500
Total fixed assets	80,000	*Total Shareholder Equity*	93,500
Total assets	**99,500**	Total liabilities and Shareholder Equity	**99,500**

Key points:
- The balance sheet reflects the state of the company's finances at a moment in time.
- Assets and liabilities/shareholder equity "balance" at all times, whether within an end of year statement or in any transaction that occurs.
- All of accounting follows the formula assets = liabilities + shareholder equity.

The Income Statement

In contrast to the balance sheet, the *income statement* (also known as a profit and loss statement, or "P&L") provides a picture of what revenues were brought into the company over a specific period of time (rather than a specific moment in time as in the balance sheet). The income statement thus represents a way to look at the operations of the company, manifest through profits or income. Some more definitions may be helpful:

Net sales: revenues obtained from sales efforts minus any returned items or discounts (such as Medicare rebates for drugs).

Cost of goods sold (COGS): overall costs for the sold product, including such things as the cost of the materials used in creating the product, along with direct labor costs and manufacturing overhead; however, it does NOT include the indirect expenses such as distribution costs, sales force costs, laboratory costs, research personnel costs, insurance costs, or other administrative overhead costs.

Selling, general and administrative expenses (SG&A): This typically includes the selling expenses of the sales force, marketing expenses, management personnel costs, as well as general and administrative expenses (often corporate) that the firm expends.

Amortization: The paying off of debt by regular installments.

Table 6.2 shows the income statement of TechCo.

Of note is that the income statement ties back to the balance sheet *via* the net income produced, which will end up on the balance sheet as either changes in retained earnings, or if distributed, as dividends. Hence, there is a direct relationship between the income statement and the equity part of the balance sheet. This makes sense, as any net income obtained due to operations creates wealth for those who invested in the company, manifest as equity. (The converse is also true; any losses due to operations destroys the wealth of those investing in the company.)

Table 6.2 Income Statement of TechCo

	20XX
Net sales	26,000
Cost of goods sold	14,000
Gross profit	12,000
Selling, general and administrative expense	3,500
Research and development expenses	2,200
Other expenses	300
Total operating expenses	6,000
Operating income	6,000
Interest expense	555
Other nonoperating expenses	200
Total nonoperating expenses	755
Income before taxes	5,245
Provision for income taxes	1,980
Net income	3,265

Key points:
- The income statement reflects a time period (*cf.* moment in time) describing revenues generated by operations.
- Profitability results from having net revenues exceed expenses.
- The income statement is linked to the balance sheet by the generation of net income which flows into either retained earnings or is distributed as dividends.

The Cash Flow Statement

As the name implies, the cash flow statement identifies both the principle sources and uses of cash within a company. Like the income statement, it is defined over a period of time, and reflects the operations of a firm. As distinct from the income statement, however, the focus of this financial statement is to understand whether sufficient cash is being generated by the operations of the company to pay both its operating and capital expenses. If a company's operations do not generate sufficient cash, starting cash (or cash generated through the sale of assets) on the balance sheet will be used. If internal cash is not sufficient, external financing (either debt or equity) is required. While there may be a number of aspects to the cash flow statement, fundamentally, the main components are related to

Table 6.3 TechCo Cash Flow Statement for Year 20XX

Cash flow from operating activities:	
Net income	3,265
Adjustments to net income to net cash from operations	
Depreciation and amortization	2,200
Other noncash expenses	200
Changes in assets and liabilities	
Increase in accounts receivable	(3)
Increase in inventory	11
Increase in accounts payable	(4)
Net cash provided by operations	5,669
Cash flows from investing:	
Capital expenditures	(12)
Sale of property, plant, equipment	2
Net cash provided by investing	(10)
Cash flows from financing activities:	
Increase in borrowing	25
Dividends paid	0
Exchange rate changes	(6)
Net cash provided from financing activities	19
Net increase (decrease) in cash	5,678

cash obtained from operations, cash obtained from investments, and cash obtained from financing. Note that most cash flow statements are comparative, i.e., they relate the *beginning of a period to an end of a period*. Table 6.3 shows TechCo's cash flow statement.

What can be seen from the cash flow statement is the relevance of cash payments. An increase in *accounts receivable* (another party *owes* TechCo, *viz.* has not paid TechCo as of yet), is *not* a cash payment, but rather a use of cash (credit) (as opposed to the income statement, where this is considered revenue). Further, an increase in *accounts payable* actually increases cash (somewhat counterintuitive – however cash will ultimately decrease once a payable is actually paid). The effect of depreciation is very important – the "depreciation effect" affects both the income statement and the cash flow statement. For the income statement, it *decreases* the net income of the firm, and thus, decreases overall tax rates the firm will need to pay, but *increases* the cash flow, since depreciation *per se* is not cash, but "use" of assets – hence, it is *not* a cash charge! A related concept is that payments are either expensed (as expenses on the income statement) or capitalized (i.e., included as capital expenditures on the cash flow statement, which are then incorporated as long-term assets on the end of period balance sheet). Long-term assets are then depreciated over their useful life. This concept is of particular importance to R&D executives, as purchases of equipment are generally treated as capital expenditures and not immediately expensed. An understanding of both internal and external appearance provides insight on how to match resources to R&D strategy.

While the interpretations of the balance sheet, income statement, and cash flow statement have other subtleties, the aforementioned provide the main components with which technical executives should be familiar. The following section will provide some additional ways to utilize information in these statements, based on comparative *ratios* meant to evaluate financial performance.

RATIOS

There are a variety of ways to interpret the information in financial statements. A key concept is that a comparison over a number of years is often a much more useful data set than a single year alone, since changes in strategy will be reflected in overall financial performance. Ratio analysis is no different; comparison over a number of years, and within industries, is of particular importance for gleaning information needed for decision making. While the judicious use of the financial statement data will improve the understanding of most R&D personnel regarding the status and strategy of a particular company or unit, it is within the context of the entire firm that these numbers should be taken into account. It is probably obvious that ratios alone are not *per se* sufficient to definitively conclude anything about a company; they are more like a single experiment amongst many, which provide a detail of the entire picture of the system. The following will describe ratios for TechCo and provide definitions of terms that the technical executive may encounter.

Financial Performance Ratios

Return on equity (ROE):
- Most popular ratio for evaluation of past financial performance
- A measure of relative efficiency of use of shareholder investment in the company
- ROE = net income/shareholder equity

In the case of TechCo,

$$ROE = 3,265/93,500 = 3.5\%$$

for year 20XX; so for every dollar of shareholder investment, the company earns $.035 of profit.

Return on assets (ROA):
- A component of ROE
- A manifestation of both the profit margin and asset turnover
- ROA = net income/assets
  For TechCo,

$$ROA = 3,265/99,500$$

or TechCo earned 3.3 cents for every dollar in assets.

Gross Margin:
- Gross margin = gross profit/sales, where *gross profit* = net sales − COGS
- COGS includes material costs, direct manufacturing labor, and factory overhead costs including factory management, utilities, rent, and depreciation.

[This is a financial accounting concept. The parallel concept in managerial finance is contribution margin, although it is used somewhat less frequently:

$$\text{contribution margin} = \text{gross contribution/sales}$$

where

$$\textit{gross contribution} = \text{Net sales} - \text{variable production costs}$$

(Variable production costs represent mainly materials used in production but also other variable costs such as outside testing.)]

In the case of TechCo,

$$\text{gross margin} = (26,000 - 14,000)/26,000 = 46\%$$

Hence, 46 cents of every sales dollar is available for R&D, SG&A (selling, general and administrative costs), other costs, and contribution to profits.

Liquidity Ratios

Liquidity represents the ability of a company to generate cash from its assets; as such, it is a short term assessment. Often, creditors will use such ratios to evaluate the relative level of cash available to pay bills and/or short term obligations (such as loans). Two frequently used liquidity assessments include working capital and the current ratio.

Working capital:
- Provides investors with an idea of the company's underlying operational efficiency and its short-term financial health.
- Typically, a positive balance indicates the ability to pay short-term debts and liabilities.
- However, money tied up in inventory and money owed to the company (accounts receivable) also increase working capital.
- Working capital = current assets − current liabilities
  For TechCo,

$$\text{working capital} = 19,500 - 6,000 = 13,500$$

Current ratio:
- Similar to working capital, measures the ability to meet short-term liabilities.
- Has similar caveats to working capital calculations regarding inventory and accounts receivable.
- Current ratio = current assets/current liabilities
  In the case of TechCo,

$$\text{Current ratio} = 19,500 / 6,000 = 3.25$$

A modification of the current ratio is the quick ratio, which is the most conservative test of liquidity; this ratio does not include inventory in the current assets (nor prepaid expenses) since these convert to cash slowly or not at all.

Turnover Ratios

These ratios measure the use of assets to generate sales; with higher turnover, financial performance of a firm improves. Note that more assets are not necessarily better for a business; generating cash from a low asset business (with low overhead, variable costs, etc.) is ideal. In most instances, assets are required to generate income for a company; it is the *efficient use of those assets* that demonstrate financial performance.

Inventory turnover:
- Reflects how often in a given time period (often a year) the inventory is sold.
- Declines in inventory turnover suggest stocking of more goods.
- Inventory turnover = COGS/ending inventory
  For TechCo

$$\text{inventory turnover} = 14,000/500 = 28 \text{ times per year}$$

So in the case of TechCo, the average item will be in inventory about 13.04 days (365 days/28 times = 13.04 days per time).

Total asset turnover:
- This ratio describes sales volume in terms of the capital investment of the firm.
- Decreases in the ratio can occur in situations where too much money is being built up in total assets; in general, with the caveat noted about comparisons over multiple years, a higher total asset turnover is better than a lower one.
- Total asset turnover = net sales/total assets
In the case of TechCo,

$$\text{total asset turnover} = 26{,}000/99{,}500 = 0.261$$

so TechCo is generating $0.261 of sales for every dollar of assets.

Leverage Ratios

Leverage is the use of debt to finance a firm's assets. Debt financing creates an obligation and recurring expense (interest), but it also adds revenue-generating assets without diluting shareholders. Because interest is an expense, evaluating leverage in a company typically revolves around using some sort of cash flow measure to determine whether there is sufficient cash flow to service debt payments (both interest and any required principal payments). Some additional definitions are useful in this regard (refer to the income statement):

EBIT:
- Earnings before interest and taxes.
- This is the standard measure of operation profit, or the profit generated from operations; for TechCo

$$\text{EBIT} = 12{,}000 - 3{,}500 - 2{,}200 - 300 - 200 = 5{,}800$$

EBITDA:
- Earnings before interest, taxes, depreciation and amortization.
- EBITDA is an important measure of the cash flow generated from operations. Bankers will generally use this number to determine a company's debt capacity; for TechCo

$$\text{EBITDA} = 12{,}000 - 3{,}500 - 300 - 200 = 8{,}000$$

Compare this to the net income of $3,265 from the income statement.

Interest coverage:
- The ratio of operating cash flow to interest expense.

- This ratio is used by bankers to quickly determine the credit of the company. A company with a high credit rating will have a high interest coverage ratio.
- Interest coverage = EBITDA/interest expense
  For TechCo,

$$\text{interest coverage} = (6{,}000 + 2{,}200)/555 = 14.77$$

showing that the company earned its interest liability over 14x in 20XX, indicating very low levels of interest payments.

Debt-to-Equity Ratio

- One of the most common measures of financial leverage.
- Measures solvency based on how much debt is being used in the capital structure.
- Debt-to-equity ratio = total debt (both short and long term)/shareholder equity
  In the case of TechCo,

$$\text{debt-to-equity ratio} = 500/93{,}500 = 0.5\%$$

This indicates that for every dollar supplied by shareholders, $0.005 is being supplied by creditors, indicating a very low degree of leverage for the company. Table 6.4 summarizes these ratios.

Table 6.4 Ratio Summaries

Financial Performance	
Return on equity (ROE)	Net income/shareholder equity
Return on assets (ROA)	Net income/assets
Gross margin	Gross profit/sales
	where *gross profit* = net sales − COGS
Liquidity	
Working capital	Current assets − current liabilities
Current ratio	Current assets/current liabilities
Turnover	
Inventory turnover	COGS/ending inventory
Total asset turnover	Net sales/total assets
Leverage	
Interest coverage	EBITDA/interest expense
Debt-to-equity ratio	Total debt/shareholder equity

COGS: Cost of goods sold.
EBITDA: Earnings before interest, taxes, depreciation and amortization.

DISCOUNTED CASH FLOW

The budgets that each executive (technical or otherwise) submits represent components of financial expenditures desired in the present where *cash flows* at some time in the future are expected to result. When company management teams make decisions to "invest" in projects or programs, they by definition choose to expend financial resources in such projects instead of interest-bearing securities or deposits; the firm will use money today with the expectation of benefits or revenues sometime in the future. Such economic consequences depict the *time value of money*, wherein a dollar today is worth more than a dollar obtained at some time in the future. Indeed, it is cash flow that is the most relevant metric for finance   while accounting treatments are relevant, as noted previously, they are backward looking, and hence do not portray the future ability to generate cash. As a result, any choice of projects or programs is analyzed by what cash value is anticipated in the future, "discounted" back to the present, and compared to the outlay of capital today (in the form of the noted budgets). This process is known as discounted cash flow analysis, or DCF. In the context of the technical executive, projects and programs are expected to generate some level of return for the company, which relies on expected revenues, often forecasted by the commercial part of the organization. Such forecasts of cash flow after R&D expenditures (usually over multiple years) then allow calculation of the overall present value of the activity for the company. This is the basis by which budgeting and forward looking financial planning is performed.

Net Present Value

Probably the most well known term used in financial valuation is net present value (NPV), and most technical executives are at least familiar with this concept. The NPV method of project evaluation uses a *discount rate* (or *cost of capital*), which is basically the rate of return that could be obtained by the company or its investors by investing elsewhere (see the section "Cost of Capital" later in the chapter). It may also be viewed as the *opportunity cost* of investing in a given project. Hence, the formula for calculating NPV is

$$NPV = \text{present value of future cash inflows} - \text{initial investment}$$

$$NPV = \sum_{t=1}^{n} [\text{cash flow}]_t / (1 - k)^t - \text{initial investment}$$

where t = time period, and k = cost of capital.

It is important to note that the dollars used in this equation are present value dollars (i.e., today's dollars) for valuations back to today. One could hypothetically calculate these to any period of time (e.g., 10 years into the future), which is done when planning for a variety of scenarios. Nonetheless, when an NPV is positive, this indicates the investment will earn a return greater than the cost of capital. Thus, a positive NPV suggests a project should go forward since it should increase the wealth of the company. The converse is obviously true; a negative NPV would result in making the company poorer, and thus should be rejected. When the NPV is zero, the company does not become richer, but does not become poorer either, and hence any investment in such a project would be marginal and should take into account other factors which might be important (e.g., opportunity cost of workers involved in other projects; maintenance of a plant to avoid mothballing, etc.).

Key points:

- The ability to generate cash from operations is the primary concern of the finance function of the company.
- NPV is a commonly used financial tool to evaluate a project (investment).
- NPV requires forecasts of initial capital required and future cash flows for projects as well as a discount rate (*viz.* cost of capital).
- NPV > 0 suggests a firm should invest in a project; NPV < 0 suggests rejection of a project; NPV = 0 requires further evaluation.
- NPV can be used to both determine wealth creation for a company as well as prioritization of projects/programs for a firm.

Internal Rate of Return

The internal rate of return (IRR) is an alternative to the NPV, and represents the discount rate equal to the present value of the cash going into the project, *viz. it is the discount rate when the NPV = 0.* Hence, using the equation for NPV, solving for the discount rate, and setting NPV = 0, one could obtain the formula for the IRR. This is no mean feat, and in general, utilizing tables or programs is the preferable method for determining the IRR in any given situation, particularly if cash inflows are different from year to year (which is almost certain to be the case).

Of note is that IRR and the NPV will usually but not always indicate the same course of action. The general rule for use is that any project with an IRR that is greater than the discount rate should be funded, wherein those that are lower should not be funded. Use of the IRR for ranking projects is challenging for a variety of different reasons, including that projects with higher initial investments will be penalized with a lower IRR (expected return), even if they have higher overall returns (and thus NPV); projects with different durations should not be compared, since

IRR does not consider cost of capital (which can be different at different times within the project's duration); there may be multiple IRRs per project, etc. The NPV is able in a relatively straightforward manner to provide information that can inform the technical executive regarding which projects will provide wealth to the firm, and will give a relative ordering of the value of each. As a result, given the challenges with the IRR, use of the NPV is preferred.

Key points:

- IRR represents the discount rate where the NPV = 0.
- There are challenges to calculating and using the IRR in mutually exclusive projects.
- The NPV provides clearer information for most situations than the IRR and is preferred in most value calculations, at least from a theoretical point of view.

Cost of Capital

The cost of capital is an often misunderstood concept for technical (and other) executives. The cost of capital, or as noted, the discount rate, is the opportunity cost the company incurs by investing in a project, as opposed to an alternative similar-risk investment. Basically, *it is the reward an investor can expect to earn for investing in a given company.* In this context, an investor can provide the company with capital today, understanding that there will be a payback in the future which needs to take into account the time value of money. There are thus two components of cost of capital:

1. A risk-free interest rate (e.g., U.S. government bonds).
2. A risk premium, which is the reward an investor will demand for a perceived level of risk.

The risk-free interest rate varies, but is generally considered to be equal to the short-term U.S. Treasury rate (typically 3-month T-bills). Historically this rate has averaged about 3–4%.

The risk premium is more difficult to calculate, and can be modified in many different ways. In general, the *market risk premium* is based on *what could be earned on average in the stock market;* while estimates vary from economist to economist, a value of 6–7% *on average* has been used in this regard. So, as an oversimplified example,

$$\text{Cost of capital} = \text{risk free interest rate} + \text{risk premium}$$
$$= 3\% + 7\% = 10\%$$

It is emphasized there are *many factors* that will affect this basic calculation, particularly, the risk premium (e.g., interest rates, leverage in the capital structure, overall market conditions, specific industry, etc.). Often, this is a weighted average of several different factors, depending on the capital structure of the firm, e.g., whether companies hold debt obligations. Table 6.5 provides formulas for calculation of the cost of capital, based on stock market models (capital asset pricing model, or CAPM) or by using the weighted average cost of capital (if debt is held). It is important for the technical executive to note that arbitrarily setting the cost of capital higher or lower magnifies the effect on the NPV calculation; *this is not a place for "gut" feelings about discount rates, or setting higher hurdle rates, as significant errors in investment can occur!* In fact, this is a calculated entity, and indeed, the cost of capital is a component of *an investment* (in a project, program, or transaction), rather than the whole company. Further, companies often may not have a single cost of capital, for instance if a larger business has different business segments, and/or operates outside the United States.

The concept of beta (β) deserves brief elaboration. In the CAPM model, β is a measure of *systematic* risk, i.e., market risk (not individual stock risk), and cannot be avoided in a given market ("economy-wide risk").

Table 6.5 Formulas Used to Calculate Cost of Capital

Cost of capital (based on the capital asset pricing model)	$r_e = r_f + \beta$ x market risk premium r_e = expected returns to shareholders r_f = risk free premium (e.g., Treasury bill return) β = the nondiversifiable (systematic) risk of an *individual* security or company compared to the market (for the market as a whole, $\beta = 1$) Market risk premium = estimated risk on average of investing in the stock market (often estimated at 6–7%)
Weighted average cost of capital (WACC) (for leveraged companies, i.e., companies with debt)	WACC = [debt% x cost of debt x $(1 - t)$] + [equity% x cost of equity] Debt% = amount of debt/(debt + equity) Cost of debt = effective rate a company pays on its current debt from the various bonds, loans and other forms of debt utilized t = corporate tax rate Equity% = 1− debt% Cost of equity = $r_f + \beta$ x market risk premium

Nonsystematic risk is firm-specific risk (not market risk), and *can* be avoided with diversification, *viz.* by holding stocks that are diversified. β only captures systematic risk in the CAPM model, since it is assumed that an investor is well diversified (see also Chapter 5 on portfolio management). $\beta = 1$ indicates that a stock has the same volatility as the overall market (and thus the systematic risk of the market); $\beta > 1$ indicates a stock with more volatility than the market (with more systematic risk than the market); and finally, $\beta < 1$ indicates a stock with less volatility than the market (and therefore a lower systematic risk than the marketplace).

Moreover, in reference to the paragraph above, a particularly important aspect of cost of capital to the company and the technical executive is what it is NOT: a hurdle rate due to uncertainty. Discount rates should *not be increased* on R&D project revenues and costs, since as noted β only measures the undiversifiable ("systematic") portion of the total risk of a stock compared to the market. Based on CAPM, research project risks are "idiosyncratic" (*non*systematic), and such risk *is* diversifiable (fully diversified investors "diversify away" this risk, leaving only systematic risk). *Hence, such technical projects do NOT affect the cost of capital.* Executives need to be very clear that uncertainty related to future R&D results and the movement of a company's stock price due to correlations to the stock market are *not* the same. The only risk affecting the expected return required by investors is systematic risk. This is important in order for companies to avoid making costly mistakes utilizing inappropriate metrics for decision making purposes, and very much indicates the challenge and relevance for interpretation of the components of NPV for technical executives.

Key points:

- Cost of capital is the overall cost of the funds used to finance a firm's assets and operations, which typically is some combination of debt and equity financing.
- Cost of capital is a calculated number which takes the following into account:
  1. A risk-free interest rate (e.g., government bonds)
  2. A risk premium based on a number of factors, including but not exclusively interest rates, market conditions, correlations with the stock market, and specific industry factors (systematic risk)
- The weighted average cost of capital is a weighted average of the cost of debt capital and the cost of equity capital used to finance a project or firm; the cost of debt capital is after tax, since interest payments are tax-deductible (and dividends are not).

- Cost of capital is often estimated for a specific investment project rather than an entire company (although it may be approximated across a firm if the projects are close enough).
- R&D project risks are idiosyncratic (nonsystematic), and should not engender a higher cost of capital; avoid confusing uncertainty of the future with risk of stock market correlations (systematic risk).

Off-Balance-Sheet Accounting

Off-balance-sheet accounting (also "off-balance-sheet financing") reflects an accounting technique in which a liability (e.g., debt) does not appear on the company balance sheet. This may make a company appear more profitable and creditworthy by potentially misrepresenting its true assets and liabilities. One way to effect such accounting is to create a "special purpose vehicle" (SPV), which represents a new company to which the assets and liabilities may be transferred. Hence, a company could create an SPV and transfer assets and debt it did not wish to carry on its own balance sheet; if the sponsoring firm wholly owned the SPV, then all of the assets and liabilities would show up on the parent's balance sheet. As a result, SPVs are typically partially owned (at most) by the parent company, particularly if being used to inflate revenues and minimize liabilities. The poster child of off-balance-sheet transactions performed to deceive investors was Enron. Amongst other things, Enron would build assets such as power plants, and by using a rationalization of consistent earnings, would book *projected* (as opposed to actual) revenues for profits; if/when the actual revenues of said plant did not meet expected profitability, and thus generated losses, the company would put the plant into an SPV and not report a loss on its own balance sheet. Ironically, at the time Enron was engaged in these businesses, many of these accounting practices were not illegal. With the collapse of the company, significant reforms were put in place to prevent such an occurrence in the future. While some off-balance-sheet transactions are both legal and desirable (e.g., lease back provisions, spin-outs), changes in accounting rules and the Sarbanes-Oxley Act now tightly regulate the disclosure of such entities by the parent companies.

GENERAL REFERENCES AND WEBSITES IN FINANCE

Bruner, R.F., Eades, K.M., Harris, R.S., Higgins, R.C., 1998. Best practices in estimating the cost of capital: survey and synthesis. Financial Practice and Education Spring-Summer, 13–27.

Gitman, L.J., 2006. Principles of Managerial Finance, twelth ed. Addison-Wesley, New York.

Higgins, R.C., 2009. Analysis for Financial Management, ninth ed. McGraw-Hill Irwin, New York.

McNulty, J.J., Yeh, T.D., Schulze, W.S., Lubatkin, M.H., 2002. What's your real cost of capital? Harvard Business Review October, 5–12.

Shim, J.K., Siegel, J.G., 2000. Financial Management, second ed. Barron's Educational Series, New York.

Business and Finance Articles, <http://www.business-finance.org>. (accessed 17 August 2012)

U.S. Department of the Treasury, <http://www.treasury.gov>. (accessed 25 July 2012)

Product Development

Table of Contents

"High expectations are the key to everything."

Sam Walton

"Nine people can't make a baby in a month."

Fred Brooks

INTRODUCTION

The product life cycle is a mainstay of the R&D process, and technical executives are familiar with many components of the tactical activities of product management prior to launch. However, there are a number of concepts involved in *marketplace* product development and ongoing product enhancements of which the R&D staff may be less familiar. These are usually under the purview of the commercial and/or corporate groups within a company. Because of the importance of these areas in maximizing the value of a product (or product line) within a firm, the technical executive should be familiar with these concepts in order to best be able to contribute to the execution and development of products and their modifications within the marketplace.

The Pragmatic MBA for Scientific and Technical Executives
DOI: http://dx.doi.org/10.1016/B978-0-12-397932-2.00007-7

PRODUCT LIFE CYCLE

The product life cycle is a model depicting various stages of product sales from initiation and launch to withdrawal from the marketplace. While not all products traverse through a defined life cycle (due to failures, competitor products being introduced, changes in the environment, etc.) it is a very helpful way of thinking about the types of challenges facing products as they move through the marketplace and into the hands of consumers. Further, the distinctions within the product life cycle can be helpful in order to plan for the types of activities needed to support programs for products as well as the response to feedback (e.g., client innovation) that may arise.

In general, there are four distinct stages of the product life cycle: introduction, growth, maturity, and decline; at each point, the profitability based on sales is different, and thus the strategic approach differs as well (see Figure 7.1). Indeed, the type of approach an organization will use for each one of the stages of a product life cycle will define its competitiveness within the marketplace (see the "Disruption" section later in the chapter), particularly since the buyers and customers at each of the stages will also vary.

Introduction

In the *introductory stage*, a manufacturer or company launches a product not previously on the market. Because this phase is associated with gaining acceptance in the marketplace, there are typically no profits generated,

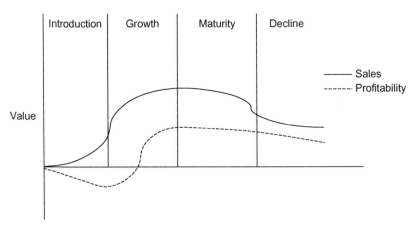

Figure 7.1 *Product Life Cycle.*

and the goal is to move through this period as quickly as possible. There is a high level of uncertainty at this time about the product, but resource intensity is necessarily high (technical, manufacturing, and engineering support is required in order to ensure product availability) and focus on *new customers* is key. Moreover, the importance of distribution partners (see Chapter 1 on Marketing) is relevant in order to drive demand from respective downstream members of the channels, including retailers and other intermediaries (depending on whether the product is commercial or industrial in nature). The relevant result is *awareness of features and the value proposition* of the product to the targeted customer group. The technical executive may encounter the terms "pioneer" and "fast follower" within the context of the introductory stage; the former relates to being the first with a product category or class, taking on higher risk with the thought of higher reward as a first mover; the latter looks to determine if a new product or class is accepted, and if so, enters into the marketplace with a product similar to the pioneer but with certain features which may allow the competing product to be distinguished. Again, this is dependent on the type of product being launched.

Growth

During the *growth stage*, there is more awareness of the product, with requisite increases in awareness, and potentially clarity in brand (i.e., brand differentiation). Profits begin to increase with sales, and there may be attraction of new market and customer segments to the product outside of the original groups. Because of the relative success, new entrants enter into the market, and marketing expenditures increase in order to compensate for the increased competition. For pioneer products, alterations in the product profile may occur, learned from lessons in the marketplace, and fast followers develop their products based on the understanding obtained by observation of the pioneer product (albeit without first mover advantage). The maximum profitability for a product is during the later part of this phase, in part because of the relative clarity on product profile, distribution channels, and cost leadership achieved with experience.

Maturity

At the end of the growth phase and beginning of the *maturity* stage, product revenues begin to plateau due to flattening of sales. As the maturity stage progresses, revenues will typically slowly fall off, and there will be a relative stability in the product demand and features during this time period. While this phase may last for some time, and can be a period of stable revenues, it is also a period of high risk, where market changes, changes in product, and changes in distribution may all create significant environmental alterations for the product franchise. In this stage, original manufacturers may begin to produce private brands for distributers and create differentially priced brands in order to capture more market share from competitors. The longer the maturity stage, the greater the chance that another product/customer solution will emerge and erode market share (see the "Disruption" section later in the chapter). The technical (and marketing) executive should be well familiar with the traits of the products that have driven success and endurance in the marketplace, and thus have plans to either provide additional features to extend the maturity phase, facilitate new product development which will allow introduction of a new product or product line which can begin a new life cycle (using lessons learned from the mature product), or divest from the marketplace. Being a cost leader with reduction of manufacturing costs can also be part of the maturity phase.

Decline

The *decline* stage is usually a manifestation of another product as superior technology and/or commercial changes in product usage, associated with reduction of sales and profits. In this stage, close attention needs to be paid to costs to match the noted loss in revenues. In this stage, a *shakeout* may occur, where weaker competitors who can no longer compete due to cost constraints leave the market, leaving behind the strongest competitors who are cost leaders. While profits may be relatively low, there still may be cash flow from limited segments (even if there is a newer version of the product on the market), which has been created by the earlier positioning of the product during the introduction, growth, and maturity stages. Usually, this stage is completed for a firm when the product is withdrawn from the market, or the product is sold to another manufacturer (see, for example, Table 3.1 in Strategy chapter).

Table 7.1 summarizes the product life cycle components.

Key points:
- The product life cycle is a model that represents a strategic view of products being developed and introduced into the marketplace.

Table 7.1 Product Life Cycle Components

Introduction	New product for the marketplace; main goal is to generate awareness
Growth	Market has accepted product; grow competitiveness and market share
Maturity	Maintain position in marketplace; take away market share from competitors
Decline	Survive shakeout by being cost leader; maintain cash flow by close attention to expenditures and unit sales

- There are four main components to the product life cycle: introduction, growth, maturity, and decline.
- Each stage of the product life cycle is associated with company activities to either shorten the stage (introductory phase, where there are limited revenues) or prolong the stage (late growth, maturity, and decline, to maximize revenues).

ADDITIONAL READING

Grieves, M., 2005. Product Lifecycle Management: Driving the Next Generation of Lean Thinking. McGraw Hill, New York.

Hines, P., Francis, M., Found, P., 2006. Towards lean product lifecycle management: a framework for new product development. Journal of Manufacturing Technology Management 17, 866–887.

Subrahmanian, E., Rachuri, S., Fenves, S.J., Foufou, S., Sriram, R.D., 2005. Product lifecycle management support: a challenge in supporting product design and manufacturing in a networked economy. International Journal of Prod Lifecycle Management 1, 4–25.

DISRUPTION (DISRUPTIVE INNOVATION)

The term *disruption* refers to the ability of smaller firms to displace larger company dominance in a certain product or product lines. This concept, introduced by Clayton Christenson in 1995, revealed the susceptibility of products in *maturity* to be replaced by innovative products, which may not have been (at least initially) well described or accepted in the marketplace. Conceptually, when products are introduced, they can be *continuous* or *discontinuous innovations*. Continuous innovations typically do not require an active change in the behavior of the customer; often products are improvements or replacements of the previously used ones. In contrast, discontinuous innovation *does* require a change in behavior, since the products are fundamentally different in the way they serve a need of the

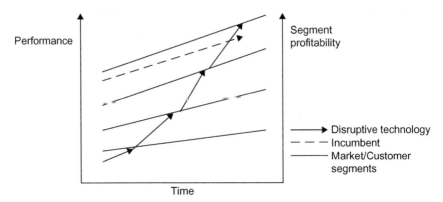

Figure 7.2 *Disruptive Innovation.* Disruptive technology enters into the lowest profitability segment, and progresses toward higher market segments by innovating to eventually displace the market leader incumbent.

customer. Similarly, Christensen described *sustaining* and *disruptive* innovation. A *sustaining innovation*, like continuous innovation, improves expected performance of existing products in solving a problem for the customer, and supports the company from which it originates. In contrast, a *disruptive innovation* may have characteristics not valued by these same customers, including being simpler, less expensive, and/or lower quality compared to current products. Nonetheless, there is a marginal or new customer segment to which the innovative product adds value, but this may be initially too small for large firms (the market leader) to consider. However, these disruptions alter an existing market by beginning to serve new customers, thus allowing a company a foothold in a market with a "good enough" product ("low-end market disruption"), which is ignored by the market leader. As the disruptive company attempts to move to higher profitability market segments, it innovates to provide a higher quality and/or more sophisticated product with more characteristics to serve the next segment (often unimpeded by others); again, this may be relatively small, and may not be a segment on which the market leader is focused. With several iterations of this cycle, the disruptive company may finally serve the most profitable segment, which then drives the market leader into obsolescence. Recognition of a disruptive technology, and response by emulation or investment, with constant pushing of product technical standards, is considered to be a useful tactic for avoiding the progression of such disruption on the incumbent company (and market leading product). Figure 7.2 shows a graphical depiction of the disruptive process.

Key points:

- Disruptive innovation occurs during the maturity phase of a product life cycle.
- Continuous innovations typically do not require change in behavior of the customer, while discontinuous innovation does require a change in behavior.
- Disruptive innovation serves a niche customer base that is less profitable from that of the industry leader, but gradually innovation from the upstart company produces a product that displaces the incumbent from its leadership position.

Inhibiting Disruptive Innovation

While there are many examples of disruptive innovation in diverse industries (from digital photography to computer hard drives), barriers can be erected (intentionally or otherwise) to prevent disruptive innovation. Indeed, this can occur by the maintenance of a standard that creates obstacles for new entrants, allowing *sustaining* innovation (from entrenched industry players). An example of this is the development of novel medical treatments; because of the regulatory rules (e.g., from the Food and Drug Administration, FDA) involved in obtaining approval for such therapies, particularly previously undescribed approaches, it is much easier for new entrants to use a pathway with which regulatory bodies are more familiar (thus decreasing the FDA's need to conceptualize new approaches using old rules). Although hypothetically a new entrant could develop a totally unique treatment for a given disease and attempt to move this through development toward approval, in fact the resources necessary are prohibitive due to the time required for such learnings by FDA, given the significant rules, regulations and general processes established by the regulatory bodies for human studies. This is particularly true for small companies who would typically be the originators of such innovations. Hence, the unintended consequence of a highly regulated system is the inhibition of disruptive innovation, and support of sustaining innovation in product development.

ADDITIONAL READING

Bower, J.L., Christensen, C.M., 1995. Disruptive technologies: catching the wave. Harv. Bus. Rev. January–February, 43–53.

Christensen, C.M., 1997. The Innovator's Dilemma: When New Technologies Cause Great Firms to Fail. Harvard Business Press, Boston.

ADOPTION AND DIFFUSION

As part of the product life cycle, the behavior of each customer in specific phases represents a *market segment*. These segments, interestingly enough, do not represent a homogeneous grouping, but different (although not exclusive) buyers entering into the introductory, growth, maturity, and decline segments. Indeed, the process by which a product spreads through buyer groups is called the *diffusion of innovation* process, and the cognitive and behavioral process a customer utilizes to purchase a totally new product is called *adoption*. The stages of the adoption process include awareness, interest, evaluation, trial, and adoption; Table 7.2 summarizes these components.

As noted, there are a number of *adopter categories*, and these are considered to be individual market segments, as each category has a similar set of characteristics. They include *innovators, early adopters, early majority, late majority*, and *laggards*. The characteristics of each group are different enough to require a different set of strategies to address their respective needs and wants.

Innovators represent the initial 2.5% of potential product adopters, and are individuals who are most likely to buy a new product. They are considered "venturesome," in that they are most likely to accept new ideas. This group is typically considered to be younger, better educated, and have higher incomes, and so can sustain the risk of adopting new products/technologies. These individuals adopt the product during the introduction stage.

Early adopters constitute the next 13.5% of buyers who adopt; the difference from innovators is that they move into the market during the growth stage, rather than the introductory stage. Similar to the innovators, this group tends to be younger, more educated, and with higher income than average; however, they also have more connections with the local community, and in particular, the next segment of adopters (early

Table 7.2 Stages of the Adoption Process

Awareness	A potential customer becomes aware of the existence of a product
Interest	The customer is aware and potentially may seek information
Evaluation	The customer seeks information and begins to (mentally) determine if the product is a solution for a problem
Trial	There is actual use of the product on a limited basis
Adoption	If the trial use at least meets expectations, the customer uses the product in preference to other potential solutions

majority). Often, such individuals are *opinion leaders*, who can shape the acceptance of products by others if their needs are satisfied.

The *early majority* is more risk averse than the early adopters, and represents 34% of adopters. This group tends to be more cautious, is of average socioeconomic status, and is more willing to wait until there is product acceptance before committing to purchase; hence, they tend to adopt during the late growth stage. Similarly, the *late majority* represents another 34%, but this group only adopts the new product because of economic or social reasons, and when the product has reached maturity. This group is more conservative, and tends to be somewhat less well educated and financially stable than the early majority.

Laggards are those in the final 16% of adopters, who only adopt a product at the very end of the life cycle. This group actively resists change, tends to have the lowest socioeconomic status, and may only adopt a product when it has already been replaced by another product.

It should be clear the different adopter groups represent very different market segments that need to be taken into account during the product life cycle. These groups consist of different marketing mix and customer segmentation challenges that technical executives should be aware of, as the strategy to address each group will be different and require different support from the R&D and marketing components of the organization. There are challenges as well with respect to a company being able to traverse each of these segments successfully, particularly with a new technical product (see the section "Discontinuities in the Product Life Cycle" later in the chapter). Table 7.3 summarizes the adopter groups.

Table 7.3 Adopter Groups

Innovators	First 2.5% of adopters; most likely to try something new; younger, more highly educated, and more financially secure; purchase at introductory phase
Early Adopters	Next 13.5% of adopters; similar to innovators, but buy product during the growth phase; more integrated into their communities
Early Majority	Ensuing 34%; more cautious but still adopts product in (late) growth phase; average socioeconomic status
Late Majority	Next 34%; older and more conservative; adopt when forced to do so by social or economic reasons during maturity
Laggards	Remaining 16%; lowest socioeconomic status; by the time this group adapts, there may be a replacement product on the market

Key points:
- The process by which a product spreads through buyer groups is called the *diffusion of innovation*.
- The process a customer utilizes to purchase a totally new product is called *adoption*, which encompasses awareness, interest, evaluation, trial, and adoption.
- Adoption of new products is diffused throughout a particular social system, and consists of different market segments: innovators, early adopters, early majority, late majority, and laggards.

ADDITIONAL READING

Rogers, E.M., 1983. Diffusion of Innovations. Free Press, New York.
Schreier, M., Oberhauser, S., Prügl, R.W., 2007. Lead users and the adoption and diffusion of new products: insights from two extreme sports communities. Marketing Letters 18, 15–30.

DISCONTINUITIES IN THE PRODUCT LIFE CYCLE

As noted above, the model of the product life cycle is a useful paradigm to create strategies and clarify approaches, depending on where the product exists within its life cycle. However, particularly in *discontinuous innovations* (see above), it is rare that the progression of stages are as clear cut or as smooth as depicted in Figure 7.1; in fact, as described well by Geoffrey Moore (1991), there are significant discontinuities within the process which should be addressed due to the differing needs of the customers in each segment. Indeed, "cracks" in the bell curve of adoption occur, particularly in high technology industries, between the *innovators* and *the early adopters*, and between the *early* and *late majority*, which need bridging for successful product adoption. However, the widest "chasm" exists between the *early adopters* and the *early majority*, since these groups have very different product needs and represent an area where a level of sophistication is required to traverse, resulting in more profitable growth for the firm. The technical executive will likely be exposed to these concepts, particularly with new products, in new product lines, and in earlier stage companies.

At the outset, the differences between the *innovators* and *early adopters* are reflected in the interests of each respective group. While the inclusion of both groups is important as an early market, the innovators tend to appreciate a technology for its own merits, while early adopters are looking to solve a business problem (not a technology goal). Hence, the early adopters look for a "strategic leap" forward, while the innovators simply want just the newest technology available. To bridge this gap, the messages to each group should emphasize different components. For the innovators, the product components that make it superior to currently available technology should be clear, and the ability to test versions of the technology should be offered if at all possible. For the early adopters, an articulation of the breakthrough to solve a key problem that exists in the business should be clearly apparent, with an invitation to reference the innovator group for the potential to execute such a vision.

The differences between the *early majority* and *late majority* have been described in the context of their adaptability to new technology. The transition between these two groups focuses on the willingness of the early majority to learn how to use a given new technology, and the lack of such a willingness in the late majority. Indeed, this lack of willingness is despite the fact that the market is already developed, minimally in late growth/early maturity. The challenge here is to transition between these stages by understanding that the early majority is typically interested in *incremental progress* from what existed previously, while the late majority is more entrenched in *mature products* which are typically *trailing edge* rather than leading edge. Each requires a messaging approach that shows the standardization of the product in the marketplace, and with maturity, the emphasis on *service* that minimizes the level of technologic sophistication needed by the late majority to use the product.

The transition between the *early adopters* and the *early majority* is of particular interest, since it represents a deep divide in the product life cycle, due to the fundamental differences between groups. The rationale put forward by Moore is that each group reviews technology in a different way. The early adopter tends to look at new technology with the belief that *their insights are the most relevant* in the evaluation of novelty and usefulness, and that their vision on the build product infrastructure is *unlikely* to include current efforts. Moreover, early adopters are thought to be interested in technology beyond their industry; they see opportunities for high technology solutions from other industries in their own industry (and vice versa). In contrast, the early majority is *looking for reference groups* whom they trust to validate the technology, and as noted previously, require *incremental innovation* rather than revolutionary changes. The emphasis is on *standardization*, with requisite support functions and ability to connect directly into their respective industries. This "chasm" is much larger than that described for innovators and early adopters and the early majority and late majority, since the needs of the respective early adopter and early majority groups are so different.

In order to address this divide, attacking a niche market is suggested, one that is either too small or uninteresting to large competitors. With that, the product may be able to establish a beachhead and (eventually) dominate this market, using it as a base for creating a reference group by which momentum can be established into larger markets (i.e., early majority). A key point of emphasis is that such an approach is applicable to discontinuous innovations; with continuous innovations, the progression relates more to the relatively continuous adoption curve depicted in Figure 7.1.

Key points:

- Discontinuous innovation is associated with discontinuities in the adoption process at the transitions from innovator to early adopter, from early majority to late majority, and most prominently, from early adopter to early majority.
- Understanding the specific needs of each of these groups is important in order to drive adoption from each and move downmarket to the largest segments.
- In the largest "chasm," from early adopter to early majority, establishing a beachhead by targeting a niche market to create dominance and a reference group allows "crossing" into the larger and more profitable markets.

ADDITIONAL READING

Moore, G.A., 1991. Crossing the Chasm. Harper Business Books, New York.
Robinson, R., Pearce, J., 1986. Product life-cycle considerations and the nature of strategic activities in entrepreneurial firms. Journal of Business Venturing 1, 207–224.

DOMINANT DESIGN

Technology design in product development undergoes significant discontinuities and uncertainties in the marketplace. During these periods of uncertainty, continued innovation and competition occur in order to establish a standard, *viz.* a dominant design. The dominant design is therefore defined as "a single architecture that establishes dominance in a product category." While dominant designs may take years to emerge, it is clear that at times none is ever established (e.g., Xbox, PlayStation, Wii). While there are studies showing that certain industry factors can drive a dominant design, more broad factors have been noted that are seemingly

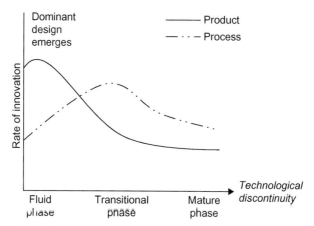

Figure 7.3 *The Paradigm of Dominant Design.* Product innovation is followed by process innovation; at the mature phase, technological discontinuity can begin anew, starting the cycle once again. *Adapted from J.M. Utterback, Mastering the Dynamics of Innovation. Boston: Harvard Business School Press, 1994.*

important. Interestingly, the apparent emergence of a dominant design is NOT technology driven, but rather a complex interplay between various players around a product category, including competitors, alliance groups, the government, and other cultural or geographic concerns. Nonetheless, the emergence of a dominant design quells the uncertainty in the product, *per se*, and as classically articulated, shifts the emphasis to *process innovation* within the dominant design. Parenthetically, classically, there is a difference between assembled products, where the product innovation is higher than the process innovations, and nonassembled products, where the opposite is true. However, the goal of process innovation is to provide incremental improvements in the dominant design, including driving down costs and improving efficiencies in manufacture (see Figure 7.3) (however, see the sidebar on the following page, "Variation on a Theme: Dominant Design and Biopharmaceuticals").

The period of incremental improvement represents an opportunity for additional technologic innovation. (see "Innovation and Economics" in Chapter 2, as noted in "Product Life Cycle" and "Disruptive Innovation" sections). Once these new technologies begin to compete within the industry and the various players, the uncertainty and discontinuity begin anew, and the process for establishment of a new dominant design ensues to replace the incumbent product. Indeed, studies have shown that the ability of an organization to substitute its own products and processes ("cannibalizing" its own products) with a new dominant design is a fundamental component of competitive advantage. This occurs in both high and low technology industries, which differ only in the time to potentially achieve dominant design as well as the time for the next technological discontinuity and emergence of a new dominant design. These concepts are very much related to the discussions on innovation, as well as (in the context of cannibalization) the concept of the ambidextrous organization (see Chapter 4).

Key points:

- Dominant design is the result of an interplay of different players in an industry, which is typically not technology driven *per se*.
- Dominant design choice by the marketplace ends technological discontinuity and shifts innovation to processes and incremental improvements.
- During the time of incremental improvements, new technological discontinuities can occur, resulting in the establishment of new dominant designs.

Variations on a Theme: Dominant Design and Biopharmaceuticals

Dominant design has typically been depicted graphically as the overlap between product and process innovation curves, with product innovation distinctly preceding process innovation. Classically, a dominant design emerges as the result of technological discontinuities that have settled on a given finished product solution. Subsequent to this market choice, the life cycle of the product undergoes process innovations in order to address costs as well as the overall product supply – it is primarily the generation of efficient processes for product manufacture. Although there may be differences in degree of innovation of the product *vs.* the process, these efforts are considered distinct in the innovation process.

This paradigm has helped clarify and explain a variety of different engineering and other scientific product innovations. It is clear, however, that there are situations where product and process innovations are (and must be) synchronized, rather than exist as sequential elements as initially described. Such an example includes the development of biopharmaceuticals. These therapeutic agents are the result of using recombinant biotechnology for manufacture of drug/drug candidates. Often, during the various stages of development, the process of providing biological material for study, whether in discovery, preclinical studies, clinical evaluation, or ultimately the marketplace, must evolve *during* the overall development of the compound. As such, the product – *viz.* the resultant protein being tested for clinical efficacy – is being developed at the same time as the process for generating the protein product itself. Hence, rather than being separate curves, the product and process curves overlap, and must do so given the need of companies to provide a consistent pathway for manufacture to submit to regulatory bodies. In this case, there is a tacit understanding that the overlap of these curves may indeed increase the risk of product development, as contemporaneous innovation is required for successful development of the product. Maintaining a separation of the product and process innovations may be prudent (if possible) to maximize the opportunity of successful product development for the marketplace.

Lim L, Garnsey E, Gregory M. Product and Process Innovation in Biopharmaceuticals: A New Perspective on Development. Center for Technology Management Working Paper Series, 2004/01, June 2004.

ADDITIONAL READING

Funk, J.L., 2002. Standards, dominant designs and preferential acquisition of complementary assets through slight information advantages. Research Policy 32, 1325–1341.

Suárez, F.F., Utterback, J.M., 2007. Dominant designs and the survival of firms. Strategic Management Journal 16, 415–430.

GENERAL REFERENCES AND WEBSITES IN PRODUCT DEVELOPMENT

Griffin, A., 1997. PDMA research on new product development practices: updating trends and benchmarking best practices. Journal Product Innov Management 14, 429–458.

Morone, J., 1993. Winning in High Tech Markets. Harvard Business School Press, Cambridge.

Tushman, M.L., O'Reilly, C.A., 2002. Winning through Innovation: A Practical Guide to Heading Organizational Change and Renewal. Harvard University Press, Boston.

Michigan State University Product Center, <http://www.productcenter.msu.edu/> Accessed 18 August 2012.

The Lean Advancement Initiative at MIT, <http://lean.mit.edu/> Accessed 18 August 2012.

CHAPTER 8

Operations

Table of Contents

"If one learns, but does not think, one is lost; but if one thinks, but does not learn, one is in danger."

Analects of Confucius

"You've got to be very careful if you don't know where you're going, because you might not get there."

Yogi Berra

INTRODUCTION

When considering the overall value chain of a respective product/ program, a particular aspect the technical executive will often encounter is the approaches to manufacturing process(es), particularly in the delivery of quality in process or final outputs. While there are many tactical and specialized considerations inherent in these outputs, there are other, broader concepts that have been described and adapted that apply to many different forms of production. Indeed, such strategic approaches are very much related to philosophical considerations of improvements in managing not only individual components of complex programs, but also the entire manufacturing and operation system through consideration of holistic approaches. In particular, an understanding of quality, and the management of quality *capabilities*, vis-à-vis the *avoidance of waste*, is an important

The Pragmatic MBA for Scientific and Technical Executives
DOI: http://dx.doi.org/10.1016/B978-0-12-397932-2.00008-9

concept that spans the operational world and has important consequences for technical professionals.

Moreover, it is the development of such capabilities and the changing mindset of employee empowerment that drives many of the operational concepts seen today in leading organizations. Such capabilities include the ability to continuously adapt and improve given processes through out the organization, in order to be able to deliver quality products that match the needs of the marketplace, and to do so in the most efficient and lowest cost manner. Such efforts require a substantial and wide-ranging degree of effort within the organization, from senior managers to those working on the production floor. Indeed, this is a distinct shift from the thinking of years ago when product defects were attributed to inadequacies of production personnel (rather than managerial efforts around processes and systems). In fact, W. Edwards Deming (the father of quality control) showed that only 15% of quality issues were due to actual production staff error; the remainder was due to issues around systems dynamics and process inadequacies (including poor management). He noted that quality improvements required organizational philosophical changes and commitment, involving all in the company, and in particular, senior management.

As noted, these fundamental operational objectives require significant efforts throughout the organization. Part and parcel of these efforts is the degree of employee empowerment and involvement in every component of the process. Characteristically, employees in high-functioning organizations, where operational excellence has been noted, are empowered to seek out problems and correct them without fear of punishment; they are the key component in the identification and improvement mechanism that ensures quality. Every employee in firms such as Toyota is an *internal customer*, receiving outputs from a process from another in the company, and thus can act as a continuing check on quality *before* products reach the *external customer*, who purchases the product. Working together, the employees of an organization with an embedded emphasis on quality are able to generate products delivered with the lowest cost and maximally meet customer needs in a timely fashion.

TOTAL QUALITY MANAGEMENT

Quality can be defined both as an internal and external concept. However, the definition of quality is as different as the number of individuals one queries – whether from the perspective of internal R&D personnel, marketing staff, or customers (as many software engineers will know intimately). Obviously, there is no universal definition; however, that does not imply that the concept cannot be used for operations excellence. Fundamentally, as a framework, quality can be considered internally as the capability to execute processes that allow for outcomes that match or exceed expectations (e.g., conformance to specifications, fitness for use), which have been defined by the customer (e.g., value for price paid, support post purchase). As a paradigm, this is a concept often used when considering the nature of quality in an organization.

Of note, like any process within a firm, trade-offs exist and resources are not unlimited when considering the achievement of quality in a company's offering. There are defined costs as part of the achievement of quality that need be considered when evaluating the depth by which quality will be embedded within an organization (see Table 8.1). Indeed, the costs of quality have been much considered since the time when the Japanese first implemented the concept of *total quality management*. Clearly, there are associated costs with poor quality – from dissatisfied customers and lost sales to internal repeated efforts. The internal costs include quality control costs (appraisal and prevention costs) as well as quality failure costs (internal and external failure costs). It is the former that need to be balanced with the latter ("cost/benefit") in order to best create a process that provides the highest quality product with the most efficient production process for the company.

Appraisal costs relate mostly to the concept of quality control: this is the set of processes used to identify product deficiencies, which includes a host of activities from in-process inspections to final product evaluation. *Prevention costs* are incurred to prevent the production of defective goods,

Table 8.1 Costs of Quality

Appraisal Costs	Costs associated with determining defects (e.g., product testing)
Prevention Costs	Costs incurred when attempting to prevent poor quality (e.g., product design cost)
Internal Failure Costs	Costs incurred to identify poor quality prior to the product arriving to the customer (e.g., rework, scrap)
External Failure Costs	Costs associated with poor product quality once purchased by the customer (e.g., warranty claims)

effected by process planning and product/process design expenditures. This can include diverse activities ranging from design review to process validation; the key is that these are proactive efforts. As noted, both appraisal and prevention costs are used in an attempt to prevent internal and external failure costs; *internal failure costs* are those associated with finding quality issues (e.g., nonconformance to specifications) prior to arriving at the customer; this may require *rework*, where the product needs to be repaired or corrected in some manner, or *scrapping*, if the product quality is so low that it cannot be reworked. Both create a significant amount of both real and opportunity cost for the company. *External failure costs* are incurred once a poor quality product arrives with the customer. These are the highest costs associated with quality, as this directly impacts the customer, and thus potentially affects company reputation, and loses revenue. Indeed, appraisal and prevention costs usually represent the lowest of the costs of quality, followed by internal failure costs, and finally as noted external failure costs.

Key points:

- Total quality management represents an organizational commitment toward processes and products at the highest level of quality.
- Quality has both internal and external components, from the capacity to produce products efficiently with well-designed processes, to products which meet or exceed customer needs.
- Costs of quality include appraisal costs, prevention costs, internal failure costs, and external failure costs (the former two are an attempt to avoid/mitigate the latter two).

Quality Management: The Cost of Failure

The production of biological proteins for therapeutic use is a sophisticated endeavor, since the engines for such production are live cells or bacteria. These require exquisite control systems, and optimized operations that are consistent, tightly regulated, and diligently followed, lest the product becomes heterogeneous to the point of becoming a different entity. Genzyme (now part of Sanofi) was a biotechnology company that was focused on rare diseases; its products included Cerezyme (for Gaucher Disease) and Fabrazyme (for Fabry Disease). In June 2009, because of issues around cleaning and sterilization, the plant trains producing these products had to be shut down due to viral contamination, creating shortages of the drugs, thus putting many patients at risk. A short five months later, not only Cerezyme and Fabryzyme but three other drugs made at the same factory were found to be contaminated, this time with particles of steel, rubber, or fiber. The Food and Drug Administration (FDA) then stepped in, and issued a "consent decree," under which the factory would essentially be under third-party management, and the company would need to meet certain milestones to show they could competently operate the plant for manufacture of product. Genzyme was also required to pay a fine of $175 MM, and in addition to lost revenues, was thought to have lost about $300 MM for reparations due to the inability to manage their own manufacturing plant.

Pollack A. Genzyme Says FDA Will Oversee its Factory, NY Times, March 24, 2010.

ADDITIONAL READING

Feigenbaum, A.V., 2002. Total quality management. Encyclopedia of Software Engineering. Wiley, New York.

Psychogios, A.G., Priporas, C.-V., 2007. Understanding total quality management in context: qualitative research on managers' awareness of TQM aspects in the Greek service industry. The Qualitative Report 12, 40–66.

Asia Productivity Organization, <http://www.apo-tokyo.org>. (accessed 16 August 2012)

VARIABILITY

While the goal of operations is to produce identical outputs, it is obvious that this is inherently not possible, despite being able to come quite close. The reason for this close-but-not-exact replicability is that all processes have *variability*, whether from (for example) the sources of raw materials, the environment in which they are constructed (which may vary, including in temperature, moisture content, etc.), and/or the operations staff involved in assembly. With variability comes *waste* and thus excess costs; hence, to produce quality products and services, it is important to understand and control variability as much as possible in order to increase efficiencies and reduce cost. In general, there are two types of variability that can affect and are important in operations processes: *common cause variability* and *special cause variability*. Common causes of variability are those factors inherent within the process or system, and they affect all those products or outputs that result from the process. These are considered random, and many are typically present at a given time; however, while each has an individual effect, the sum of these common causes is typically constant (and relatively small). Examples of common causes include variation of timing of machine maintenance, variability in wire diameter, or differences in moisture content of column resins. This type of variability reflects a "stable system of chance causes" (Walter Shewhart; see Deming, 1986) and is the statistical variability of a given process or product.

In contrast, *special causes of variability* are more transient in nature, and typically affect only some products from the process. While common cause variability has several sources with small effects (which are more difficult to find), special causes are more variable with less frequency but measurable effects [*viz.* an *assignable* cause, using Demling's definition (1986)]. These are not intrinsic to the system, but are typically external; examples include desiccation of product due to placement next to heaters in the warehouse, upgrades in (incompatible) software, or intermittent power failures. As such, these can be discovered and (hopefully) eliminated from the process, most often by the operations staff or supervisors working with the process.

The treatment(s) of common and special causes of variability are different. Since common cause variability is due to numerous small and difficult to identify causes, and often due to chance, significant efforts are required to decrease it. Without changing the system or process, common cause variability will often remain "stable"; indeed, processes are considered to be stable (or *in-control*) if it is determined that common causes are present, and no special causes are influencing variability of process outputs or measures. Special causes of variability are, as noted, often detected by operations personnel and supervisors intimately familiar with the process. Moreover, use of *control charts* and *statistical process control* (both of which display and analyze information about each step of the process) can help differentiate between the two types of variability.

Key points:

- Variability exists in every process.
- There are two types of variability, common cause variability and special cause variability.
- Common cause variability is an inherent part of the system, and has many sources of small amounts of variability.
- Special cause variability is external to the system, and has more limited sources but causes higher degrees and magnitudes of variability.
- Use of control charts and statistical process control can be helpful in determining the difference between common cause and special cause variability.

ADDITIONAL READING

Acosta-Mejia, C.A., 1998. Monitoring reduction in variability with the range. IIE Transactions 30, 515–523.

MacKay, R.J., Steiner, S.H., 1997a. Strategies for variability reduction. Quality Engineering 10, 125–136.

CONTINUOUS IMPROVEMENT

In some businesses, products and processes undergo a significant amount of planning to achieve a specific metric or target. Once that target is achieved, often the respective processes are "locked" and remain fairly static, due to a variety of different factors (e.g., regulatory requirements, resource constraints). However, in *Total Quality Management*, process improvements are never "complete," but are dynamic and are constantly being reevaluated in the context of a cycle of improvements; one "completion" is the start of another cycle of a continuous and relentless search for a better process/product and further decreases in variability. Much of the advances in continuous improvement originate from the Japanese, wherein continuous incremental improvements were found to be the most lasting and beneficial to the organization (*"kaizen"*). By continuing the cycle, the company creates learnings that can be used for further improvements throughout the organization. This concept of never-ending improvement is the basis of many quality programs, including lean operations, plan–do–study–act (PDSA), and Six Sigma. The technical executive should have a familiarity with these concepts, particularly when involved in later stage product development.

Lean Manufacturing

Although originally an inventory management system, today lean manufacturing ("lean") is a systematic approach to manufacturing management, emphasizing the elimination of waste. Within lean, waste is defined as those activities utilizing resources but creating no value ("work for no value"). As noted, waste is related to variability, and thus can be seen throughout the value chain, from production to inventory management to distribution. Lean approaches attempt to make operations as consistent as possible by decreasing complexity in process flow, thereby reducing costs, and allowing identification of the sources of variation and improving quality. Using concepts such as local production, constant levels of production, small lot sizes, short lead times, as well as frequent resupply (and thus strategic relationships with limited suppliers) and integrated design and manufacturing cycles, lean operations when present throughout an organization minimize waste and the cost of producing quality products.

While there are many versions of lean today, all derived from the original Toyota Production System, technical executives may encounter some specific conceptual aspects that are common in operations. These include Just-in-Time (JIT), Value Stream Mapping, Production Leveling, and Supplier Rationalization. For a more detailed and historical discussion of lean operations, see De Feo and Barnard (2005).

JIT is a fundamental component of lean manufacturing, and conceptually reflects the idea that inventory is waste. By reducing in-process inventory, companies reduce carrying and other hidden costs of inventory keeping. Less efficient processes require more inventory and supplies to be kept on hand, to deal with inadequacies in the production process, such as process variability, machine reliability, lack of planned capacity, or one-dimensional labor. Since JIT processes require replenishment only when needed in downstream operations, processes must be well-defined in order to ensure that production is not adversely affected by stock-outs.

JIT relies on sets of symbols (e.g., "tickets") to demonstrate the need for materials of a downstream process. Feedback loops with such symbols are used to demonstrate need for replenishment at each step of the process, or if a process includes a final product, replenishment after the last step. Hence, JIT emphasizes minimization of the number of replenishment steps required to ensure efficiency. Ideally, no in-process inventory is used within the system flow, with replenishment occurring only when needed for a downstream process. With variability in demand, however, it is rare that a process will have no safety stock to avoid stock-outs, and it is expected at least some inventory will be maintained; nonetheless, conceptually, minimizing the carried inventory is an important aspect of JIT, and individual companies will need to weigh risk and opportunity costs when determining the level of safety stock carried. In addition, process simplicity (or at least minimization of complexity) is an important component of JIT processes. Given the concept of reduction of process inventory, it is apparent that a requirement of JIT is significant cooperation of the company with its suppliers, since at a minimum frequent resupply will be necessary. Hence, a systemic strategic relationship with suppliers is key in order for JIT to work well in any firm (see also the discussion of extended enterprise in Chapter 3).

Value Stream Mapping is a concept of utilizing maps of design flows, most often across multiple processes, and typically, at a systems level. There are connections made between both physical steps and the flow of information, and metrics are defined (e.g., lead time) in order to ensure connectivity with process flow. There are several variations of the classic value stream mapping techniques, and such activities have been moved beyond manufacturing to a myriad of other industries (e.g., software development, logistics, and healthcare); however, the primary goal is to recognize the steps in the value chain by visualizing the components to identify waste, unnecessary steps, or other process inadequacies. Examples of systems that can be used include a build-to-the-standard form (see Shongo, 1985) and the Design System Matrix (Eppinger, 2001); both of these can be utilized by drawing out processes by hand, or by using more sophisticated software tools.

Production Stream Leveling revolves around the production of in-process intermediates at a constant rate in order to ensure predictability of manufacturing outputs. This is a process that attempts to reduce variation in output, supply, and inventory in order to minimize waste − by keeping processes at a level rate, a company can reduce fluctuations in supplier and in-process inventory, thus minimizing costs. Because such fluctuations create waste, batch production is limited to the *smallest number of units possible*; this allows the earliest processes in production to minimize resources expended (efforts of employees, holding of inventory) until required by demand. Clearly, both production schedules and order lead times must be consistent in order for such a manufacturing flow to occur. Ideally, production can be leveled to provide uniform levels of product from the manufacturing process; however, in the real world, demand is not constant, and hence, other techniques are associated with Production Stream Leveling, such as Demand Leveling, and keeping some limited inventory, particularly at the end of the process. *Demand Leveling* relates to the use of tactics to moderate customer demand. This can include for example promotional efforts, alternations in launch times of new products, modifications of the supply chain, or use of small finished goods inventory. The goal is to create a predictable level of demand for the product, which will thus allow clarity at the level of manufacture so that required outputs can be met efficiently in a timely fashion with high quality products.

Supplier Rationalization refers to the management of suppliers, particularly decreasing the number of suppliers to ones with which the company has, ideally, a strategic relationship; this includes improved communication, with detailed information necessary to fulfill the needs of both the company and supplier and decrease risk (e.g., detailed forecasts and capacity information, respectively). The benefit of these efforts is short lead times with frequent deliveries and limited inventory (both from suppliers and in-process), which minimizes costs. It has been noted in a variety of studies that the more suppliers a company uses, the more difficult it is to implement lean operations; on the other hand, it is also clear that true partnerships are required when decreasing supplier numbers, lest the company take on supply risk because of unforeseen (or foreseen but uncommunicated) events, particularly with key components.

Key points:

- Lean manufacturing is a mindset that focuses on creating smooth process flow and minimizing waste.
- The concept of Just-in-Time is a cornerstone of lean, and reflects the emphasis of minimizing inventory by constant feedback loops and formalized identification of downstream needs in a process.
- Value Stream Mapping is a tool of lean, and is the visual depiction of a given process or system to identify waste or discontinuities that generate process inefficiencies.
- Production Stream Leveling is used to reduce variability in output, supply, and inventory.
- Supplier Rationalization minimizes suppliers to those able to provide materials with short lead times, frequent deliveries, and minimal inventory.

ADDITIONAL READING

Deming, W.E., 1986. Out of Crisis. MIT Press, Cambridge.
Naylor, J.B., Naim, M.M., Berry, D., 1999. Leagility: integrating the lean and agile manufacturing paradigms in the total supply chain. International J of Production Economics 62, 107–118.
Worley, J.M., Doolen, T.L., 2006. The role of communication and management support in a lean manufacturing implementation. Management Decision 44, 228–245.

Plan-Do-Study-Act Cycle

PDSA is one of the most frequently used tools for continuous improvement, and was derived by both Deming and Shewhart (see Deming, 1986) in the middle of the twentieth century and then modified in the 1990s. Each of these activities allows the incorporation of continuous improvement in overall operations, and is useful in other improvement efforts in contexts beyond manufacturing as well. Figure 8.1 shows the PDSA cycle. Of note is that as designed, continuous improvement never ends, as following the act Stage, the Plan Stage begins anew.

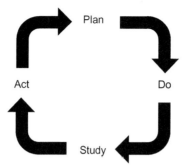

Figure 8.1 *Plan-Do-Study-Act Cycle.*

In the *Plan Stage*, the evaluation of a process is performed in order to determine if a problem exists, the degree of improvement needed and the metrics by which an improvement (if any) will be measured. A paramount consideration is the ability to measure outcomes – the nature of the issue and the measure for planned improvement must be clear in order for the ensuing stages to be successful. Key performance indicators may be evaluated at this point to utilize in the planning process.

The *Do Stage* represents the execution of the plan, with collection of data, measuring of outputs, and documentation of all modifications in the process made for further analysis in the future.

The *Study Stage* (known as the "Check" Stage prior to the 1990s) evaluates the measures made, and determines whether the plan achieved the desired metrics. Moreover, both pragmatic and logistical considerations can be made during this stage, with defining of the degree of process improvement and the difficulty implementing the changes (from feedback of staff and/or supervisors). While failure at any stage of the cycle will result in misinformation, this stage in particular has the ability to determine the relative fidelity of the data (or if inaccurate, propagates the consequences in ensuing stages).

The *Act Stage* is defined by the Study Stage (and earlier) results; the company acts upon the data that was generated and interpreted from the cycle. This involves understanding the relative success (or failure) of the efforts during the previous stages, and whether implementation or modifications need to be made. As part of this stage, any changes made must include process review to ensure that these are sustainable, with appropriate metrics and key performance indicators. The cycle repeats thereafter. Table 8.2 summarizes the PDSA cycle.

Table 8.2 Plan-Do-Study-Act Cycle

Stage	Activities
Plan	Identify which process(es) need improvement, including why, how much and how; determine metrics of measurement of process changes/improvements
Do	Execute plan, with collection of data and measurements determined in the Plan Stage
Study	Assess process improvements *via* predetermined metrics; evaluate soundness of data collection, study parameters, and validity of data; determine whether changes identified were sufficient and implementation pragmatic to recommend
Act	From conclusions garnered from the Study Stage, determine appropriate course of action; include measures of sustainability of process changes; begin Plan Stage

PDSA: A Learning Organization

Often PDSA will start on a small scale, in order to garner learnings to build incrementally knowledge that can subsequently be used on a larger scale. For example, a supervisor is looking to improve employee safety by attendance at the regularly scheduled Friday floor safety meetings.

Plan: Supervisor asks floor managers at one plant if they would like more information on strategies to improve attendance at floor safety meetings.

Do: Supervisor addresses floor managers on Monday at a single plant to determine if they would like more information.

Study: Floor managers interested; supervisor encouraged by response.

Act: Supervisor monitors meeting attendance on Fridays as initial metric, with plan to monitor safety issues over ensuing month.

By using PDSA, the floor managers may be able to increase attendance at safety meetings, and thereby decrease safety-related issues at the plant; if successful at the initial plant, this learning can be implemented at other plants by having supervisors address floor managers similarly (i.e., plan again). PDSA thus creates a learning organization by creating a hypothesis, identifying metrics, analyzing the data, and assessing subsequent activities by articulating such learnings and determining the necessary next steps required for each process being studied.

ADDITIONAL READING

Srivannaboon, S., 2009. Achieving competitive advantage through the use of project management under the plan–do–check–act concept. J General Management 34, 1–20.

van Tiel, F.H., Elenbaas, T.W.O., Voskuilen, B.M.A.M., Herczeg, J., Verheggen, F.W., Mochtar, B., et al. 2006. Plan-do-study-act cycles as an instrument for improvement of compliance with infection control measures in care of patients after cardiothoracic surgery. Journal of Hospital Infection 62, 64–70.

Six Sigma

Six Sigma, derived from the statistical aspects of process capability, is a quality improvement methodology and business strategy emphasizing the *prevention* of defects (as distinct from the detection of defects). As noted, the term Six Sigma relates to quality performance, where there are no more than 3.4 defects per million iterations, and relates to *reduction of variation and waste* by a company-wide culture. While there are tools encompassing the Six Sigma platform, it is a true *cultural shift* that must include all of a firm, from production line staff to senior managers, in order to be successful. Typically, Six Sigma encompasses the use of dedicated teams, which have been trained in statistical methods and are intimately familiar with given processes within the firm; as such, these teams have the ability to review and improve upon such processes to (as much as possible) eliminate defects. Engagement of all levels of the company is an important aspect of Six Sigma, wherein executive leadership creates the vision and allocates the resources, and creates roles for others within the organization (champions, master black belts, black belts, and green belts; see Table 8.3). By defining such a system, executives (and the company) show their dedication to the quality function as one that cuts across the organization as a key capability.

Six Sigma methodologies can be considered to be at least partially derived from the PDSA Cycle described by Deming and Shewhart. Two common ones described include *DMAIC* (Define, Measure, Analyze, Improve, Control) and *DFSS* (Design for Six Sigma). DMAIC is

Table 8.3 Roles in Six Sigma

Group	Role
Senior Management	Develop vision and allocate resources
Champions	Typically derived from senior management and oversee implementation of Six Sigma across firm
Master Black Belts	Coaches of Six Sigma; identify projects for Six Sigma evaluation; all time dedicated to Six Sigma
Black Belts	Dedicated to projects in which Six Sigma is being applied; operate under Master Black Belts; all time dedicated to Six Sigma
Green Belts	Trained in Six Sigma implementation but continue other job responsibilities

frequently used by companies incorporating Six Sigma into their business strategies; the process is primarily implemented for those products/processes/programs that *already exist within the firm*, with the overall goal of improving such activities. Similar to PDSA, the *Define Phase* of Six Sigma is essentially the Plan Stage; the Six Sigma team defines the problem and creates a plan ("project charter") by which activities and metrics will be assessed; the *Measure Phase* relates to the Do Stage of PDSA; this is the collection of data and measurements articulated in the Define Phase. The *Analyze* and *Improve Phases* relate to the Study and Act Stages of PDSA; data is evaluated, and steps are created to address the defined problem; finally, the Control Stage explicitly defines the need to perform process reviews to ensure sustainability of gains noted earlier in the process.

DFSS is a process that uses the appropriate quality tools early in product development to achieve high quality initially, and is designed for *new processes/outputs* for the company. DFSS utilizes many tools that are important in quality product design [e.g., probabilistic design, DFQ (design for quality)]; there is an emphasis on *new value* creation, and hence more attention to customer and business needs. DFSS often will utilize the DMADV process (Define, Measure, Analyze, Design, Verify):

Define: Define goals consistent with customer demands and firm strategy

Measure: Measure and identify characteristics critical to quality and risks

Analyze: Evaluate and design alternatives and processes

Design: Perform and optimize design

Verify: Verify the design and production process

Key points:

- Six Sigma reflects a business strategy and methodology for quality that emphasizes prevention of defects.
- The Six Sigma methodology requires engagement of all aspects of the organization, from senior executives to production line staff, and represents a cultural dedication to these quality measures.
- The DMAIC (Define, Measure, Analyze, Improve, Control) methodology is used for continuous improvement of existing processes/products within the company.
- The DFSS/DMADV (Designed for Six Sigma/Define, Measure, Analyze, Design, Verify) methodologies relate to products or processes that are new to the company.

Lean and Six Sigma: Air Force Smart Operations 21

When the Air Force was evaluating opportunities for process improvement for higher quality and performance around operations, senior members found that utilizing lean and Six Sigma concepts, which promoted eliminating steps, minimizing inventory, and improving quality control and tolerances, was the approach needed to become more efficient in the "journey for self-improvement." As an example, key metrics that were addressed included faster turnaround of aircraft by optimizing workflow using "work cells," where tools and parts were made available to local workers within the cell (to avoid travel to access the materials away from the airplane), rolling supply bins for commonly used parts, and "vending machines" to provide parts on an as-needed basis to avoid warehousing and inventory. Other aspects re-engineered included inspections of aircraft, where the flow of the process was changed from a sequential, serial process, where discovered issues were only addressed after every functional group had evaluated the aircraft, to one where multiple processes could occur in parallel, allowing identification of any long lead time items that could be addressed right away, instead of waiting to the end of the serial process.

Air Force Smart Operations 21 has been identified as the cornerstone strategy for improvement of the Air Force's product development process. Within the first year, these efforts resulted in reduced rework and flow days to such a significant extent that it was awarded the Silver Medal of the Shingo Prize for Operational Excellence.

Lopez, CT. Air Force improving production with Smart Operations 21, Air Force Print News, 1/9/2006.

ADDITIONAL READING

De Feo, J.A., Barnard, W., 2005. JURAN Institute's Six Sigma Breakthrough and Beyond – Quality Performance Breakthrough Methods. McGraw-Hill, New York.
Goffnett, S.P., 2004. Understanding Six Sigma: implications for industry and education. J Industrial Technology 20, 2–10.
Kwak, H.Y., Anbari, F.T., 2006. Benefits, obstacles and future of Six Sigma approach. Technovation 26, 708–715.

SUPPLY CHAIN COORDINATION: INFORMATION SHARING

With efficiencies derived from various systems in continuous improvement, the movement of products through manufacturing to the consumer has also evolved. This supply chain management encompasses ensuring the meeting of demand as accurately and in as timely a manner (as well as profitably) as possible, despite having different partners/companies responsible for each specialized role (see also Chapter 1 on Marketing). Today, this is a highly orchestrated and facilitated process, achieved particularly through information sharing. Indeed, this has evolved from the older system of two-way information flow between suppliers, plants, distributors, logistics providers, and customers, to seamless access where all relevant parts of the supply chain can share real-time information though a centralized database, updated by all involved parties. This has been made even easier with minimal increases in marginal costs by web-based interfaces, and modeling using tools such as collaborative planning, forecasting, and replenishment (CPFR) software. Such IT approaches have become *de rigueur* in the development of supply chains in a whole host of retail and specialized industries.

The type(s) of information that have high impact in supply chain efficiency vary by industry, but some consistencies do exist. Timeliness of information is an absolute necessity if it is to be of value for supply chain management, as is a high level of detail. Again, most software packages can be configured in order to provide the level of detail desired for other members in the chain, although clearly a fundamental understanding of a company's competitive position will dictate that which can be shared and what should remain confidential. Nonetheless, at least information around sales, inventory, production scheduling, fulfillment data, forecasts, demand planning, and sourcing planning, are important to consider in coordinating a supply chain (and when considering supply chain partners).

For the technical executive, decisions that should be considered for supply chain coordination include the degree and extent to which (*viz.* how many stages) throughout the chain a given company should share information. While different industries clearly have different demands and aspects of their supply chain, studies suggest sharing information *to a significant extent* (between manufacturing, distribution, and retailers) provides the maximum benefit and reflects the lowest cost within the chain. Moreover, in other studies, inventory was found to be minimized with maximal information sharing; high variations in demand magnified the benefits. Hence, while it may not be possible to include all supply chain members in the information sharing paradigm, there are clear benefits, at least in some industries, showing that diverse information sharing is a key component of supply chain coordination and driving profitability.

Key points:

- The supply chain represents the interconnected businesses involved in moving a product to the customer.

- Coordinating the supply chain takes considerable effort, best managed by the sharing of information amongst partners for lowest cost and highest profitability.
- While industries differ, there are key informational components that can have a major impact on the smooth coordination of the supply chain that should be considered, including timeliness and level of detail of information to be shared.

ADDITIONAL READING

Huang, Z., Gangopadhyay, A., 2004. A simulation study of supply chain management to measure the impact of information sharing. Information Resources Management Journal 17, 20–32.
Lau, J.S.K, Huang, G.Q., Mak, K.L., 2002. Web-based simulation portal for investigating impacts of sharing production information on supply chain dynamics from the perspective of inventory allocation. Integrated Manufacturing Systems 13, 345–358.

GENERAL REFERENCES AND WEBSITES ON OPERATIONS

Beckman, S.L., Rosenfield, D.B., 2008. Operations Strategy: Competing in the 21st Century. Boston, McGraw-Hill Irwin.
Eppinger, S.D., 2001. Information at the speed of innovation. Harvard Business Review 79, 149–158.
Reid, R.D., Sanders, S.R., 2007. Operations Management: An Integrated Approach, third ed. John Wiley & Sons, New York.
Shongo, S., 1985. A Revolution in Manufacturing: The SMED System. Productivity Press, London.
Spear, S., 2009. The High Velocity Edge. McGraw-Hill, Boston.
Lean Enterprise Institute, <http://www.lean.org>. (accessed 17 August 2012)
The Lean Edge, <http://theleanedge.org/>. (accessed 17 August 2012)
National Institute of Standards and Technology, <http://www.nist.gov>. (accessed 17 August 2012)

CHAPTER 9

Business Law

Table of Contents

"A judge is a law student who marks his own examination papers."

H. L. Mencken

"In law, nothing is certain but the expense."

Samuel Butler

INTRODUCTION

Business law encompasses the components of the legal system required or impacting the operations of the business. For the technical executive, many facets of the legal system are familiar, since they influence the day-to-day activities of the company; intellectual property and contracts are clearly some examples with which most executives have had some sort of experience. While having legal counsel is often appropriate and necessary for a variety of activities, business decisions should be framed around solid business principles and guided by the law, rather than the other way around. Indeed, effective management requires both a fundamental understanding of key legal concepts, and use ethical of judgment to execute a sound business strategy. For both the technical and nontechnical executive alike, such an understanding is key to being forthright in action, and rigorous in commitment, without fear of the legal ramifications of company activity.

CONTRACTS

As most professionals are aware, contracts are basically agreements between parties ("making law" between parties, with certain constraints). Within this context, contracts act not only to bind parties to an agreement, but also describe how such agreements will be enforced. It is axiomatic that such agreements should be entered into voluntarily, with an understanding that the resultant contract reflects an agreement in which the (self-) interests of the parties have been articulated and understood. Typically, there is also "consideration" that is involved, defined as something of value, to be exchanged.

The enforcement of contracts is *via* the courts, and the law provides the guidelines by which contractual agreements can be created (e.g., in order to avoid exploitation, issues of preemption [contrary to federal law] or public policy, and the like). Parties that do not act within the bounds of a contract are said to have "breached", and can be sued in court for "relief" to be granted from the party that breached to the nondefaulting party. If the breach is not so egregious that it may be addressed, such remedy is called "curing" the breach. "Damages" can be awarded (a monetary sum) to the nondefaulting party as compensation for a breached contract. However, if the courts decide that relief cannot be redressed by damages alone, they can institute other types of action, such as "injunctions," where a party must refrain from certain actions (e.g., selling in a market) or "specific performance," wherein a breaching party is required to perform a specific act (e.g., payment of royalties). Both of these are considered "equitable remedies" (as opposed to damages). The technical executive should note that, particularly in commercial agreements, these are not issues of "right" and "wrong"; they are a matter of either performing to the specifications articulated or agreed in the contract, or paying damages or performing equitable remedies. In contracts, then, there is no punitive aspect.
Key points:
- Contracts are agreements between parties that bind such parties to both the agreement and its respective enforcement.
- In cases where there is a breach of contract, the courts enforce the contract and provide damages to the nonbreaching party.
- Where the courts decide that damages are insufficient redress for the breach, the courts may institute equitable remedies, including injunctions or specific performance.
- There is typically no punitive component in a contract.

Contract Breach and Punitive Damages?

On August 13, 1999, City of Hope National Medical Center (City of Hope) sued Genentech (a biotechnology company) for breach of fiduciary duty and for breach of contract, based on Genentech's development of a licensed recombinant DNA technology from City of Hope. At issue was whether there was a fiduciary duty (i.e., duty to act in the best interest of another) between two contracting parties. At the first trial, the jurors could not reach a verdict, and the case was retried in June 2002, where City of Hope obtained a judgment against Genentech for breach of fiduciary duty and for breach of contract. The judgment awarded City of Hope more than $300 million in compensatory damages and $200 million in punitive damages. Genentech appealed, ultimately to the California Supreme Court, who found no fiduciary relationship existed between Genentech and the City of Hope through the licensing agreement between the parties. As punitive damages cannot be awarded for a breach of contract, the court removed the jury award of $200 million in punitive damages to City of Hope, leaving the $300 million in compensatory damages (and $175 million in interest).

City of Hope Nat. Med. Center v. Genentech, 181 P. 3d 142 – Cal: Supreme Court 2008.

ADDITIONAL READING

O'Brien, D., Hamilton, N.D., Luedman, R., 2005. The Farmer's Legal Guide to Producer Marketing Associations (An Agricultural Law Research Publication). Drake University Agricultural Law Center, Des Moines.
Poole, J., 2010. Casebook on Contract Law, tenth ed. Oxford University Press, New York.
Plain English Guide to Contracts, <www.business.gov>. (accessed 23 June 2012)

TORTS

The law of torts is based on the context of *duty*; individuals have interests that the law protects that are not based on contracts (verbal or written) or agreements. These are more social obligations, where the failure of duty to respect such interests is a "tort." Examples of these interests in tort law (i.e., protected by tort law) include areas as diverse as trespass (violation of interest of controlling access to one's home or work) to assault (violation of interest to be free of harmful touching). Table 9.1 provides examples of some interests protected by tort law.

Table 9.1 Examples of Interests Protected by Tort Law

Violation	Tort
Violation of control of disclosure of one's environment or activities	Invasion of privacy
Violation of control of access to home/business	Trespassing
Violation of reputation	Libel (written defamation), slander (spoken defamation)
Violation of bodily integrity	Assault (threat of touching), battery (actual touching)
Violation of protection from consumer product defects	Product liability

For the technical executive, this broad area of the law is particularly important, as it covers many divergent areas such as employment law (see the section "Employment Law" later in the chapter), product-specific claims that may arise, fiduciary duties that arise (*viz.* acting in the best interest of another, e.g., the corporation), and issues of "nuisance" (harmful/harming/annoying activities, e.g., noisy factory) and restraint of trade (prevention of the ability to do business). A particularly relevant concept for the technical professional in tort law is the "standard of care." While occurrences and accidents may occur within daily company activities, not every one of these episodes is subject to tort liability. Indeed, if such activity meets an appropriate standard of care (e.g., what a "reasonable person" would consider appropriate to prevent others from harm), then the occurrence would not be considered in violation of tort law. These evaluations are done within a particular context of the occurrence, and reflect a complexity around potential scenarios that could occur. "Negligence" is said to have occurred in cases where a standard, such as the reasonable person standard, has *not* been perceived to have been met. Importantly, while negligence may not be intentional, there is still assignment of fault.

Key points:

- Tort law is concerned with the duty to act in a fashion respectful of specific obligations, and when violated, results in particular injury or loss.
- The standard of care is an important concept within tort law; the "reasonable person" standard is an example of the application of this concept, and when this is met there is no violation of tort law.
- Negligence is said to occur when a given standard is not met, regardless of whether intentional or not.

Product Liability

Product liability can be evaluated in contexts that are tortious and those that are not. Negligence, as noted previously, results from not meeting an applicable standard of care, with the inherent assignment of fault. *Warranties* are statements about a given product and assurances that such statements are true (over which one may seek redress if that is not the case). Warranties are considered *contracts*, and contract law typically applies. In contrast to both of these types of product liability, "strict liability" is tort law that a manufacturer is responsible for certain types of harm *without* demonstration of fault, *viz.* despite the fact there was no intent to cause harm and a reasonable standard of care was used to prevent harm. In this case, there is only the requirement that a tort occurred, and a responsible party was identified. It is important, however, to understand that the harm was due to a *defect* in the product (rather than the inappropriate use of the product). Additionally, in strict liability punitive damages can be awarded if it is found that a manufacturer was aware of the defect *before* harm occurred. This constantly evolving area of tort law is one the technical executive should be very familiar with, in order to understand various ramifications to product development as well as product support.

Key points:

- Product liability can fall under the purview of either tort law or contract law.
- Warranties represent a contract between manufacturer and purchaser, regulated by applicable contract law.
- Strict liability is a constantly evolving area of tort law where manufacturers are liable for defects where neither negligence nor intent is established but a tort has occurred due to a manufactured product.

Product Liability and Preemption: Name Brands vs. Generics

In 2009, Diana Levine filed a personal injury case against Wyeth (a pharmaceutical company), for a failure to adequately warn of potential adverse events due to the administration of a drug (Phenergan) by the IV-push method. Wyeth argued that federal law, *via* the Food, Drug, and Cosmetic Act and Food and Drug Agency (FDA) drug labeling laws, preempted state law for adverse event warnings. The U.S. Supreme Court ruled that in this case, federal law does not preempt state tort law for the duty to warn.

In 2011, in the consolidated cases of Pliva, Inc. v. Mensing and Actavis, Inc. v. Demahy, Gladys Mensing and Julie Demahy were prescribed the generic version of metoclopramide, to treat digestive problems. After several years of taking the generic drug, both women developed a neurological condition called tardive dyskinesia, an involuntary movement disorder. The women separately sued Pliva and Actavis, using similar arguments found in Levine v. Wyeth, *viz.* making state law inadequate warning claims, wherein the metochlopramide label failed to adequately warn of the risk of tardive dyskinesia. Pliva and Actavis argued, similar to Wyeth, that the federal Food, Drug, and Cosmetic Act, along with FDA regulations that oversee the entire drug approval *and labeling* process, preempt Mensing and Demahy's state law claims, since it was impossible to comply with both. Indeed, the generic versions of the drug required use of the *same labels as the brand name drugs*, since "federal statutes and FDA regulations required them to use the same safety and efficacy labeling as their brand-name counterparts." The Supreme Court agreed, noting that the FDA's own interpretations of its regulations included the need for identical labeling. As a result, in contrast to name brand product producers, generic drug manufacturers cannot be held liable under state tort law for not changing the label of a generic version of a drug to include new safety information.

Walker, EP. Supreme Court Rules for Generic Drugmakers on Labeling Issue, MedPage Today, June 24, 2011.

ADDITIONAL READING

Glannon, J.W. The Law of Torts: Examples and Explanations, third ed. Aspen Publishers, New York.
Shavall, S., 1980. Strict liability versus negligence. J. Legal. Stud. 1, 2–3.
FTC Bureau of Consumer Protection, <www.ftc.gov/consumer.shtm>. (accessed 11 June 2012)

INTELLECTUAL PROPERTY

As technical professionals are well aware, intellectual property (IP) is the coin of the realm around which many companies work; it is a reflection of the level of innovation and also the way businesses are protected within many technologically oriented industries. Patents fall under the purview of federal law, and in fact, are mentioned in the Constitution of the United States, "to promote the progress of science and useful arts." As such, patent law arises as part of the very fabric of the United States, and worldwide represents a common metric by which companies protect their inventions. Of note is that the America Invents Act ("Leahy-Smith America Invents Act") has and will dramatically revise the original laws around patenting in the United States, and put them more in accordance with worldwide standards. Much of the following discussion revolves around U.S. law, but the overall requirements in other countries are similar, although certainly expertise in non-U.S. regions should be sought when filing in other geographies of the world.

The basic requirements for patents in the United States are articulated in the U.S. Patent Act, in that they must be statutory, new, useful, and non-obvious; these are very similar to the requirements in other countries. By statute, the U.S. Patent Act states that processes, machines, articles of manufacture, and compositions of matter or any useful improvement of prior art are patentable. The "new" and "useful" descriptions are key, in that patentable inventions must have *both* components. New (or "novel") in this context implies that it is not previously known, and "useful" indicates the invention has a useful purpose, including operativeness. Of note is that patents will not be issued for abstract ideas, laws of nature, or human organisms, if known by the public or described in a publication or used publically (offered for sale more than one year prior to the filing date in the U.S.; in other countries, filing must occur before publication). In the past, the U.S. used a rule of first to *invent*, in distinction to first to *file*, which is the case in most other countries. Within the America Invents Act mentioned earlier, the U.S. will fall into line with most (if not all) other countries in the world using the first to *file* precedence rule. The concept of nonobviousness refers to that perceived by a practitioner engaged in the art with "ordinary skill," and is often an area of controversy; whether an individual might deduce a given conclusion based on prior experience and patents (prior art) is a very difficult determination. During the process, there is no explicit protection of a patent pending (but again, at least there is priority based on having filed a patent application).

Filing patent applications using single applications for multiple countries has been made possible by two acts, the Patent Cooperation Treaty (PCT) and the European Patent Convention (EPC). The PCT allows for the submission of a single application to apply for a patent to multiple member countries simultaneously, which process the application for patentability *individually* (the PCT does not issue the patents but rather the individual members do). In contrast, the EPC is also a single application (to the European Patent Office, or EPO) that both processes and examines the application for patentability. If the application is found to

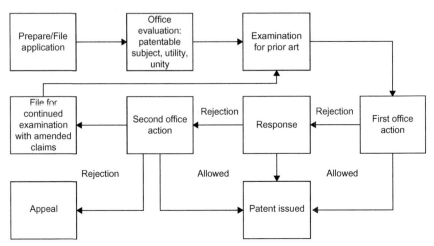

Figure 9.1 *Patent Application Pathway (U.S. Patent and Trademark Office).*

be patentable, a European patent is granted, and must be registered in the independent national offices to be valid and enforceable in each country. Each of these pathways, combined with individual country national filings, are options for patent applications, balancing cost, timing for subsequent applications, and geographic diversity desired.

Once a patent is issued, the rights associated with the granted patent are *exclusionary*, i.e., patent holders are allowed to exclude others from making, using, or selling. The rationale for this language is related to the fact that most patents are built from other patents. If an issued patent gave the right to make, use, or sell, it could potentially give the right to infringe an earlier patent. The current system thus makes patent holders dependent (potentially) on the rights of others. Regardless, the term of the patent is generally 20 years from first date of application.

Figure 9.1 shows the general process of patent processing, using the United States as a paradigm.

Key points:
- Patents in general represent novel, useful, and nonobvious inventions.
- Given changes in U.S. law, virtually all countries in the world now use the priority standard of first to file (as opposed to first to invent).
- Filing strategies encompass individual country national filings, PCT and EPC/EPO filings, and combinations thereof based on strategies around cost, territories, and planned timing.
- Patents are exclusionary in nature.

Time Delay Wipers and an Admission

Dr. Robert Kearns was awarded three patents for the invention of the intermittent windshield wiper system (the first in 1967); by report, this was based on an accident that injured his left eye, which made the constant movement of the wiper blade of automobiles of the day uncomfortable for him. When he approached the major automobile manufacturers (Ford, Chrysler, and General Motors), only Ford pursued this innovation. After receiving and reviewing a prototype, however, he was told the company was no longer interested in the device. Nonetheless, two years later, Ford's new line of cars had an intermittent wiper on their cars, reminiscent of the prototype that they had reviewed with Kearns. Kearns confronted and then sued Ford (1978), and while offered various small and larger sums of money to settle, he refused until Ford would admit that he was the rightful inventor of the intermittent wiper (1990). Subsequently, Kearns won his case against Chrysler, but lost cases against Mercedes and GM (due to late filing of paperwork). The Kearns story was made into the film, "Flash of Genius" (2008, Universal Pictures; Spyglass Entertainment).

Schudel, Matt. Accomplished, Frustrated Inventor Dies, Washington Post, February 26, 2005; Page B01.

ADDITIONAL READING

Warcoin, J., 2008. Intellectual property. Nature Reviews Drug Discovery 7, 369.
America Invents Act USPTO website, <www.uspto.gov/americainventsact>. (accessed 1 July 2012)
World International Property Organization, <www.wipo.int/about-ip/en/>. (accessed 17 August 2012)

EMPLOYMENT LAW

In general, employment law deals with the rights of employees, and ensuring that the bargaining powers of employers and employees are balanced. This area is governed by both state and federal law, with the latter preempting the former (i.e., when in conflict, federal law displaces state law). The National Labor Relations Act (NLRA) governs the employer/employee relationship, as well as interstate commerce, and regulates most of companies who do business across state lines. However, states also extensively regulate the employer/employee relationship, particularly where the NLRA does not apply.

Employment at Will

All states but Montana have allowed employers to adopt at-will policies, which provide the option to fire an employee at any time for any or no reason (and, similarly, employees may leave a company for any and no reason). In fact, most states assume that employees are hired at will, unless explicitly stated otherwise. This is a very broad law, but the employee still maintains rights in this arrangement. In particular, all but the smallest employers are subject to federal and state laws prohibiting job discrimination, and as a result, employees cannot be fired because of certain characteristics, such as race, religion, or gender, as well as age or sexual orientation. Employee contracts also cannot be terminated by reporting safety violations, discrimination, harassment, or illegal actions to company officials. Further, exercising legal rights, such as the right to take family and medical leave, to take leave to serve in the military, or to take time off work to vote or serve on a jury are not grounds to fire an employee, nor is complying with the law or filing a workers' compensation claim. Finally, firing an employee to avoid paying compensation earned either in equity or cash is also illegal. Both citizens of the U.S. and green card holders are protected, as are those who are abroad working for a U.S. domiciled company.

In addition, contracts can be written to provide specific exceptions to at-will employment. In this case, conditions can be modified such that certain time periods can exist prior to being an at-will employee, or specific aspects of the employment would be applicable for the at-will clause. Moreover, at-will contracts can also have severance agreements, where the at-will status is in effect, but if the employee is terminated without cause, or due to specific causes (e.g., company purchase) certain payments are made ("severance payments"). Hence, there is wide latitude on both employment at will, as well as modifications of such by contractual agreement.

Key points:

- Employment at will refers to the policy that employers may fire employees for any or no reason.
- Virtually all states have allowed for employment-at-will policies, noting that employers may refuse to hire an employee if they do not sign an at-will agreement.
- Employees are protected with at-will employment by federal and state laws, including those preventing dismissal due to discrimination, refusing to break laws, exercising legal rights, complying with the law, or filing a workers' compensation claim.

At-Will Employment and the Public Policy Exception

While at-will employment is accepted in virtually every state, at-will policies cannot contradict established public policies articulated by the state. The initial case that established this public policy exception was in California, *Petermann v.*

International Brotherhood of Teamsters. In this case, Peter Petermann was hired by the International Brotherhood of Teamsters ("Teamsters") to be a representative agent for the union, and was told as long as his work product was satisfactory that he would remain employed. However, he was subpoenaed by governmental agencies during his tenure with the Teamsters, who were evaluating potential corruption within the union. Against the explicit direction of his employer, he answered truthfully during his testimony, and as a result, was fired the subsequent day. He sued the Teamsters, and the California appellate court found for the plaintiff, noting that public policy limitations on at-will employment covered scenarios that had the 'tendency to be injurious to the public or against the public good'. Since lying under oath (as well as directing an employee to lie under oath) is illegal, and perjury especially in the case of governmental proceedings has large implications on public policy (despite the ability to prosecute criminally), using the public policy limitation was thought to be a more efficient and salient mechanism to execute the California laws against perjury.

Muhl, Charles J. (2001) The employment-at-will doctrine: three major exceptions. Monthly Labor Review, 124:3–11.

ADDITIONAL READING

Dannin, E., 2007. Why at will employment is bad for employers and just cause is good for them. Labor Law Journal 58, 5–16.

Miles, T.J., 2000. Common law exceptions to employment-at-will and U.S. labor markets. Journal of Law, Economics, and Organization 16, 74–101.

Stone, K.V.W., 2007. Revisiting the at-will employment doctrine: imposed terms, implied terms, and the normative world of the workplace. Industrial Law Journal 36, 84–101.

Workers' Compensation

Employers are required to furnish a reasonably safe working environment, with appropriate equipment, guidelines, and instructions as well as competent supervisors. Laws around workers' compensation vary by state, but revolve around the concept that an employee is eligible to receive certain benefits due to suffering an injury or injuries on the job. This may include medical care, rehabilitation, wages, or other payments. Companies are typically required to carry workers' compensation insurance, either issued by the state or some other carrier. Of note is that the negligence and fault of either the employee or employer is not at issue, but rather, the goal is the return of the employee to work as quickly as possible at lowest cost to the employer. Indeed, these types of occurrences exempt the employee from suing the employer who is providing the workers' compensation for the injury, although the employee may still sue any third party whose negligence may have contributed to the injury. This is truly an *employee* benefit, as independent contractors are typically not eligible for workers' compensation benefits.

In distinction to the previous paragraph, there are cases in which an employer could have anticipated, or was frankly aware, that an employee could suffer injury performing a job unless specific actions were taken for safety, but neglects to take such action. Such an employer would be liable for *willful misconduct*. Indeed, willful misconduct may not allow recovery under workers' compensation laws. Conceptually, willful misconduct can generally be considered more than negligence or gross negligence, and indeed, may be potentially criminal.

Key points:

- Workers' compensation is the eligibility of employees to receive certain benefits if injured on the job.
- All states require workers' compensation insurance to be covered by employers, either from state-funded or private insurers.
- Workers' compensation laws prevent employees from suing employers for such injuries, although employees may still sue third parties whose negligence contributed to the injury.
- Workers' compensation laws may not apply in cases of willful misconduct.

ADDITIONAL READING

Edwards, C., 2010. Public sector unions and the rising costs of employee compensation. Cato Journal 30, 87–115.
Guyton, G.P., 1999. A brief history of workers' compensation. The Iowa Orthopaedic Journal 19, 106–110.

GENERAL REFERENCES AND WEBSITES WITH ARTICLES ON THE LAW

Bagley, C.E., Dauchy, C.E., 2011. The Entrepreneur's Guide to Business Law. Thomson/South-Western, Mason.
Findlaw, <http://www.findlaw.com>. (accessed 17 August 2012)
Legal Information Institute, <http://www.law.cornell.edu/lii/about/about_lii>. (accessed 14 July 2012)
Liuzzo, A., 2012. Essentials of Business Law, eighth ed. Career Education, New York.
Nolo, <http://www.nolo.com>. (accessed 17 August 2012)

EDUCATIONAL VIDEOS

Marketing	Marketing Cases	http://www.youtube.com/watch?v= zrGOBdVm-KE&feature=related (accessed 19 August 2012)
	Marketing Strategy	http://www.youtube.com/watch?v= wAZtjhlnbdM&feature=related (accessed 12 August 2012)
Economics	Business and Economics	http://video.mit.edu/watch/business- and-economics-7621/ (accessed 7 June 2012)
	Inflation and Recession	http://video.mit.edu/watch/the-us-and- the-worlds-recession-9365/ (accessed 12 March 2012)
Product Development	New Product Development	http://www.youtube.com/watch?v= 3NjH9U_5S8k (accessed 12 July 2012)
Management and Leadership	Creativity	http://video.mit.edu/watch/7-from- ridiculous-to-brilliant-why-we-play-at- work-7596/ (accessed 12 June 12)
	Innovation	http://www.youtube.com/watch?v= gk4w-coFzRE&feature=related (accessed 7 March 2012)
	Motivation	http://www.danpink.com/video (accessed 19 August 2012)
Strategy	Five Forces	http://tv.insead.edu/video/Strategy/9/ 4127 (accessed 2 February 2012)
	Portfolio Matrix	http://www.youtube.com/watch?v= XK_rLg2f4-o&feature=related (accessed 18 March 2012)
	Core Competencies	http://www.youtube.com/watch?v= WfP-VICbLRA (accessed 2 February 2012)
	Delta Model	http://video.mit.edu/watch/1-professor- arnoldo-hax-how-does-the-delta- model-differ-from-traditional-strategic- planning-module-3885/ (accessed 8 May 2012)
Portfolio Management	Portfolio Management	http://www.tvprojectmanagement.com/ project-management/a-lean-approach- to-portfolio-management/ (accessed 19 August 2012)

Finance and Accounting	Financial Modeling using Venture Capital and Cleantech	http://www.youtube.com/watch?v= NJfvkFDxus0&list=UU4D2Z98caYHa SisrVog8aLA&index=57&feature= plpp_video (accessed 11 April 2012)
	Future of Finance	http://video.mit.edu/watch/lunch-and-keynote-address-the-future-of-finance-6878/ (accessed 18 June 2012)
Operations	Inventory and Variability	http://techtv.mit.edu/collections/ lgo/videos/11816-inventory-and-variability-dr-stanley-gershwin (accessed 12 January 2011)
Business Law	Law for the Entrepreneur	http://www.youtube.com/watch?v=Zi35 ExWyrTw&list=UU4D2Z98caYHaSisrV og8aLA&index=50&feature=plpp_video (accessed 22 February 2012)

PODCASTS

London Business School Podcasts – discussions on specific areas and thought leaders

Entrepreneurship & Business Course by Prof Mark (also at http://www.talkshoe.com/talkshoe/web/talkCastCustomAds.jsp?masterId=13431&cmd=tc) – introductory business course (taught through Carnegie Mellon University)

NPR Planet Money – good simplified explanations on different economic issues

Center for Entrepreneurial Learning – Entrepreneurs and Experts Podcast Series – practical advice on general topics in business

INSEAD Knowledgecast – pragmatic business topics

Note: Page numbers followed by "*f*", "*t*" and "*b*" refer to figures, tables and boxes respectively.

Printed and bound by CPI Group (UK) Ltd, Croydon, CR0 4YY

08/05/2025

01864770-0001